What do the other players in the National Hockey League think about superstars Bobby Orr and Bobby Clarke?

Which teams will challenge the fighting Philadelphia Flyers for the Stanley Cup in 1974-75?

What are the chances of the Houston Aeros capturing their second straight World Hockey Association title?

These and many other questions are answered in this handy, information-packed book that will help every hockey fan stay on top of the action for the entire 1974-75 season. There are hundreds of facts about all the star players, a team-by-team analysis of all clubs in the NHL and WHA . . . and much, much more!

Loaded with action photos and complete statistics, every page contains revealing, entertaining insights on the stars and the teams.

HOCKEY 1975 STARS AND RECORDS
is a hockey fan's best friend!

HOCKEY '75
STARS AND RECORDS

HAL BOCK

PYRAMID BOOKS NEW YORK

For Mom and Dad
They were superstars before anyone thought up the word.

The author wishes to commend Frank Brown of The Associated Press, John Halligan of the New York Rangers, and the National Hockey League and World Hockey Association for their help in the compilation of material found in this book.

Pyramid Communications, Inc., 919 Third Avenue, New York, N.Y. 10022

HOCKEY 1975 STARS AND RECORDS
A PYRAMID BOOK

Pyramid edition published December, 1974

ISBN 0-515-03601-3
Library of Congress Catalog Card Number: 74-11872
Printed in the United States of America
(graphic design by anthony basile)

CONTENTS

THE OPENING FACEOFF

Every hockey game starts with a faceoff, so it stands to reason that a book about the world's fastest game should begin the same way.

Once upon a time, John Kieran, an author of considerable repute, wrote an ode to his favorite sport. It was a poem called, "Give Me Hockey—I'll Take Hockey Anytime!" It was perfectly proper for Kieran to declare his love for this game in verse, because, at its best, hockey is a kind of poetry on ice.

There is a style and a grace about this sport. Call it charisma. Hockey has awesome speed, sometimes frightening body contact, excitement at every turn. And yet, intermingled with the obvious and necessary violence of the game, is something beautiful, something poetic.

The poetry is Bobby Orr, changing speeds while skating almost the way an automobile shifts gears. The poetry is Tony Esposito performing a goaltender's ballet, sprawling this way and that and somehow keeping the puck out of his net. The poetry is Bobby Hull charging up ice, his legs pumping like pistons, and drawing back his stick for an awesome slap shot that whistles towards the goal at some 120 miles per hour.

That's what hockey's all about. The heroes have changed. They were names like Howie Morenz, Lester Patrick and Eddie Shore when author Kieran wrote his ode. Now they are names like Bobby Clarke, Yvan Cournoyer and Brad Park. But the essence of the game is the same—speed and grace. It is an essence that has captured the imagination for decades past and will for decades to come.

Now, before we drop the puck, just one more thing. Give me hockey—I'll take hockey anytime!

Hal Bock
Mineola, N.Y.

PROFILES

GERRY CHEEVERS

Stationing yourself in front of a hockey net and daring the other guys to shoot that frozen hunk of rubber past you requires a rather unique frame of mind. Gerry Cheevers qualifies.

Cheevers is the veteran goaltender of the World Hockey Association's Cleveland Crusaders, acknowledged as the new league's best netminder. He jumped to the WHA from the Stanley Cup champion Boston Bruins in the summer of 1972, a couple of weeks after terming reports of the impending move "ridiculous," and "untrue."

With the WHA staging almost daily raids on the National Hockey League during the summer of 1972, any contact between the new league and an NHL player was big news. Invariably those contacts leaked out. That's how the word got around that Cheevers was talking with Nick Miletti, boss of the Cleveland club.

"This is ridiculous, unreal," complained Cheevers when the reports were relayed to him. "The story is absolutely untrue. As far as I'm concerned, I don't want to leave the Bruins. The Bruins are the best team in hockey."

Then, shortly after slamming the door on the WHA, Cheevers opened it a crack. The number being kicked around in jump rumors was $500,000.

"Where do they get these figures?" raged Cheevers. "A half-million dollars isn't even close to what I'd want to leave Boston for."

Obviously then, there was some dollar figure that Cheevers would leave Boston for. Miletti was determined to find it and it didn't take him long. Cheevers' vehement denial had come in July, 1972. Less than one month later, he announced that he was, indeed, jumping. It wasn't so ridiculous and it turned out to be quite real.

Cleveland Crusaders goalie Gerry Cheevers crayons stitch marks on his mask everytime he stops a puck with it.

"There were a thousand reasons saying I would jump, but at the same time, there were about 900 reasons telling me why I should stay with the Bruins," explained Cheevers with impeccable goaltender logic. "I weighed every possibility carefully for three to four weeks and came to realize that the move was the best thing for me and my family. I have more security with the Crusaders. My position here is very sound and that's important to me. When it got down to basics, every time I weighed a factor that I considered important to me and my family, it came up in favor of Cleveland. I'm very glad I did what I did and I'm 100 percent content right now."

So are the Crusaders. Cheevers has led the offensive-minded WHA in shutouts in each of the league's first two seasons and turned in very respectable goals-against averages of 2.83 and 3.03. He was the league's best goalie in its first season, earning a $4,000 WHA bonus for his efforts. Last year, he was No. 2 in netminding statistics behind Houston's Don McLeod.

Was Cheevers' jump reversal surprising? Not to those who know Gerry best. He can always be counted on to produce the unexpected. There was, for example, the time he was breaking in with the Bruins.

Boston was a consistent cellar-dweller in the early 1960s and the Bruins' games were usually rather lackluster affairs. One night Cheevers was in the goal and Boston surprisingly staked him to a 2-0 lead against the Chicago Black Hawks. Up in the stands, General Manager Hap Emms was thoroughly enjoying the unaccustomed prosperity. It was, however, short-lived.

The Black Hawks came roaring back and drove 10 goals past Cheevers. With each one, the fans surrounding Emms heckled the GM with a little more zest. By the time the game ended, Emms' neck was a deep red. He rushed down to the Boston dressing room.

As the GM burst into the room, he found the players downtrodden after the loss, beginning to strip off their equipment. Cheevers still had his bulky pads strapped in place and was closest to the door when Emms entered the room. He was the first player the GM saw.

"Gerry," stormed Emms, "Whatinhell happened out there?"

Cheevers looked up wearily, a trace of a smile on his lip. "Well, Hap," he began, "it was like this. Roses are red, violets are blue. They got ten and we got two!"

Speechless, Emms wheeled and bolted out the door, mumbling something to himself about goalies being crazy. Cheevers would be the first one to agree with that assessment.

"You don't have to be crazy to be a goalie," he once suggested, "but it helps."

Cheevers became a goalie out of necessity. He was playing for a CYO team in his home town of St. Catharines, Ont. His father was the coach and one day the regular goaltender failed to show up. Cheevers inherited the pads. "My dad didn't have the nerve to ask anybody else to play goal," he said, "so he put me in there. I got beat, 17-0."

It was a less than auspicious start of a career that has gotten considerably better since. Cheevers' play improved and he drifted into Toronto's vast amateur network that constantly fed first-rate prospects to the Maple Leafs during the 1950s and 1960s until the universal amateur draft ended the practice. Toronto's top affiliate was St. Michael's College and it was while he was there that Cheevers deserted the nets briefly. He moved up to left wing for a few games. The experiment was an immediate disaster.

"I almost got killed," he said. "All the guys on the other teams who were mad at me, maybe because I took a goal away from them, started to take runs at me. I'm lucky I survived."

Cheevers quickly retreated to the safety of the nets but crafty Punch Imlach used that little episode to try and sneak his goalie through the NHL's intra-league draft. Teams are allowed to protect only two goalies in the draft and Imlach wanted to keep his regulars, Johnny Bower and Terry Sawchuk, on Toronto's list. But then what would he do with Cheevers, the good-looking young prospect who was eligible for the 1965 draft. "Simple," declared Imlach. "Cheevers will be on the protected list at left wing."

It was an intriguing idea but Clarence Campbell, president of the NHL, blocked it, ruling that Cheevers was, as everybody already knew, a goalie.

Boston claimed him and Cheevers moved up to the NHL. In those days, most goalies played bare-faced, Cheevers included. But it didn't take Gerry long to discover the mask. He put one on shortly after joining the Bruins and now he wouldn't think of skating out on the ice without one. "It is a goalie's best friend," he said.

How important is Cheevers' mask? He makes sure he won't forget because everytime he stops a shot with it, he crayons stitch-marks on the face covering. "That reminds me of the scars it has saved me," Cheevers explained. There is one problem with his art work though. After four years or so of crayoning, he is running out of blank spaces for new stitch marks.

Cheevers, whose main off-ice interest is in owning and training race horses, spends most of his spare time at race tracks. "I've always loved horses," he said. "My home is filled with replicas of them."

On the ice, Cheevers is hardly a classic goalie. He improvises in the net and he's the first one to admit that.

"I fall, stand, skate a lot," he said. "I'll leave the cage to clear the puck to a forward. I've been known to skate to the blue line to start a play. I'm quite unnatural. I figure, it's not how you stop the puck, it's how many you stop."

Cheevers will get no argument with that philosophy of netminding. He's certainly made it work for him.

BOBBY CLARKE

The way Bobby Clarke was studiously avoided in the first round of the National Hockey League's amateur draft in June, 1969, you'd think he had bad breath. Actually, he had something much worse as far as the assembled hockey people were concerned. His statistics in the Western Canada Hockey League were impressive enough but there was a black cloud hanging over this youngster with the choir boy smile. It was labeled "Diabetic."

Hockey is no leisurely game. Players dash madly around the ice for 90 or so seconds at a time, sit down for a couple of minutes and then are back at it again. It is no place for someone with a questionable medical dossier. And so as the assembled NHL clubs dipped into the amateur grab bag in 1969, each of them passed up Bobby Clarke. Despite leading the WCHL in scoring in his last two years with Flin Flon, Clarke was ignored. Montreal picked Rejean Houle and Marc Tardif in the first round. Boston came up with Don Tannahill and Frank Spring. Ernie Moser, Jean-Pierre Bordeleau, Dennis O'Brien, Rick Kessell, Pierre Jarry and Jim Rutherford all were picked off and still Clarke and his diabetes remained.

Philadelphia, which had chosen someone named Bob Currier on the first round, went into a high-level huddle when its turn came on the second go-round. Scout Gerry Melnyk was urging the selection of Clarke, his medical history notwithstanding.

"It was a gamble," said Bill Putnam, president of the Flyers at that time. "We discussed the boy for days. But we felt he was the best young player in Canada, and when our doctors assured us that—under a watchful eye—he could stand up to the grind, we grabbed him."

So, on the second round of the 1969 draft, Clarke became

Bobby Clarke (16), captain of the Stanley Cup champion Philadelphia Flyers, plays hockey despite diabetes.

the 17th player chosen, and the property of the Philadelphia Flyers. Every so often, the Flyers consider how close they came to missing him. It is a frightening thought because in the draft class of 1969, Clarke was the finest hockey player available. And he proved it in very short order.

Clarke knew he had a problem. Diabetes is not something one can simply ignore. But he also knew that the medical problem need not render him helpless. There had to be a middle ground and with the help of trainer Frank Lewis, Clarke found it.

''Bobby passed out twice in our first training camp,'' said Lewis. ''But both attacks followed morning workouts when he had skipped breakfast. If there's one thing an athlete needs, diabetic or not, it's a good, solid breakfast. But Bobby knows now that we've got to be frank with each other. I'm not out to make a big project out of it when he needs something, but we both know we've got to work together on this thing."

It became daily routine for Bobby to inject himself with 55 ccs of insulin each day. "Bobby doesn't like to eat chocolate bars before a game because they make him thirsty," Lewis continued, "but I always carry some in my bag anyway. Usually, I put two or three spoonfuls of sugar into a cup of soda and he drinks it down before every game. I also have a tube of glucose that I'm supposed to jam down his throat, but that's just in case of an emergency."

Other than those precautions—the insulin, the sugar-spiked soda and the glucose tube that Lewis has never had to use—Clarke is just another one of the boys. Except for one small thing. He is easily the most talented of the Broad Street Bullies.

He started with a moderately successful rookie season of 15 goals and 31 assists for 46 points. He increased those totals to 27 goals and 63 points in his second season, then 35 goals and 81 points in his third year. That was the year the Professional Hockey Writers Association voted Clarke the Bill Masterton Award. The qualities recognized by the Masterton Trophy are "perseverance, sportsmanship and dedication to hockey." Clarke was a popular winner.

He responded with a sensational 104-point season in 1972-73 that earned him an even more important award, the Hart Trophy given annually to the National Hockey League's Most Valuable Player. Did Clarke deserve the award over, say Boston's Phil Esposito, the perennial scoring champion, who had 26 points more than Clarke, or Bobby Orr, who as usual was in a class by himself among defensemen? Flyer General Manager Keith Allen answered that question.

"I'd hate to think where the Flyers would be without Clarke," he said. "I know where they'd be. He's a leader. Everybody on this team respects him for it."

It wasn't only that Clarke was the Flyers' best offensive threat. There was the matter of his awesome penalty killing for a team that draws an enormous number of penalties.

There was the matter of his work on the power play. And there was, of course, his leadership in the dressing room. He was named captain of the Flyers in 1972, at the age of 23 the youngest player ever to wear a "C" in NHL history.

When Fred Shero took over as coach of the Flyers, he was assured by club followers that Clarke was suffering through a slow start. "You mean," he said, "he can go better than he is?" Sure enough, Clarke did pick up his pace and Shero marveled at the young center. "If I were still playing," the coach said, "I'd give half my salary to play with Clarke. He works so hard, he makes it easy for the rest of the guys."

When the Flyers realized just how good Clarke could be, they tied him up into a long-term contract, insuring against his surfacing in the rival World Hockey Association. The numbers were something like $500,000 for five years and in this era of record-breaking salaries, the figures seemed low. Clarke shrugged at that suggestion.

"How much money does one man need?" he asked. "I'm happy if I can take care of my family, have a nice house and things like a nice car, be with my friends, play hockey and swim and play some golf in the summer."

As the Flyers evolved into a rough and ready franchise, Clarke seemed to pick up that mean streak you find in all the best hockey players. A few well placed jabs with the stick got Chicago's Stan Mikita upset one night. "I don't think Clarke even knows that he's doing it," said Mikita, who's never been mistaken for little Lord Fauntelroy either. "It's probably subconscious."

"Boy, he's changed his style," noted Scotty Bowman, coach of the Montreal Canadiens. "He didn't slash like that in his first year."

They say that hard times help build character and Clarke endured his share with the Flyers. In his rookie year, Philadelphia missed the playoffs on the season's last day, beaten 1-0 on a 100-foot shot by Minnesota's Barry Gibbs. "I still see that in my sleep," said Clarke, shaking his head sadly. Then, in 1972, needing only a tie in the last game of the season to nail down a berth, the Flyers were beaten by Buffalo on a goal scored, incredibly, with only four seconds to play. "Nothing like this ever happened in 100 years of hockey," said Clarke, crying in the hushed dressing room.

But Clarke wouldn't let those disappointments destroy him. If he could overcome diabetes to play in the NHL, he could overcome those terrible breaks.

So out of the debris of those failures, the Flyers began turning things around. They finished second in the West in 1973 and threw a king-sized scare into Montreal before bowing in the playoff semifinals. Then came the West title last season and the charge to the Stanley Cup. It didn't come easy. Boston won the first game of the final Cup series and was leading Game Two with less than a minute to play. But Clarke dug the puck out of a corner and set up Moose Dupont's tying goal. In overtime it was Clarke, who seemed never to leave the ice for a rest, who scored the game-winner, the goal that turned the tide for Philadelphia.

"Bobby leads by his actions, not his words," said teammate Ross Lonsberry. "He keeps going all the time and never seems to tire."

Perhaps goalie Bernie Parent summed it up best.

"When you think of Bobby Clarke," said the goalie, "you think of hustle."

There was a time when 11 other NHL teams thought of Bobby Clarke and then thought of diabetes. It is a tribute to the captain of the Flyers that today few remember he carries that disease with him.

YVAN COURNOYER

Beep-Beep!

Yvan Cournoyer is the Roadrunner. He beats you with his speed. He is not awesomely big and not fantastically strong. But don't challenge the Roadrunner to a race. You'll lose.

"I have no idea how fast I can go," he once admitted quite matter-of-factly. "Once in training camp they timed me, but I don't remember how fast I went."

There was, however, one thing the handsome Frenchman did remember. "Offhand," he said, "I can't think of anyone who skated faster than me."

That's perfectly understandable because very few skaters in the National Hockey League can keep up with Cournoyer, who zooms up and down the right side of the ice for the Montreal Canadiens as if he had miniature jets installed in his skates.

Cournoyer possesses not only lightning speed, but has a powerful shot and some elusive fakes to go with it. The combination can be devastating. Once Bruce MacGregor of the New York Rangers was given the assignment of shadowing the Roadrunner. MacGregor analyzed the job this way.

"You have to stick by him, never let him get the jump. If he gets a step on you, he's gone. You'd need a lasso to catch him."

Another time, a rival coach was asked about Cournoyer. "The only way to stay with him," the coach said, "would be if you broke both his ankles. Even then, I'm not sure he wouldn't beat you."

Cournoyer is cagey. He often hangs out near the blue line, waiting for a pass that will spring him up ice. He needs very little time to reach full acceleration. His legs churn feverishly and he bears down on the goalie with his eyes flashing. There is a definite similarity to another Montreal right winger of

Yvan Cournoyer (12) had another 40-goal year last season. He's hit that figure four times for Montreal.

another era—Maurice Richard. Jean Beliveau, longtime captain of the Canadiens, noticed it too.

"Yvan Cournoyer and Rocket Richard are the two fastest skaters I have ever seen," said Beliveau, now a Canadiens' official. "The key to Yvan's skating is his ability to get a quick jump. He has such strong legs. The muscle development above the knees is amazing. That is where Yvan gets his quickness. The speed with which a skater can flex and unflex his knees with a kicking action is important. Yvan is very good that way. He can put on bursts of speed that can carry him past an opponent before the opponent realizes what has happened."

Beliveau centered for Cournoyer in the Roadrunner's early days with the Canadiens. "He is such a good skater that he can free lance all over the ice and still be where he is supposed to be on any given pattern. He will often go from one side of the rink to the other on a rush, but I have learned to keep track of him," said Beliveau.

In those early days with the Canadiens, Cournoyer was only an occasional player. He was a power play specialist, allowed on the ice only when Montreal enjoyed a manpower edge. There were two reasons for that. One was Cournoyer's speed, which made him an asset on the power play. The other was his defensive play, which was somewhat suspect.

As a result, Cournoyer often would languish on the end of the bench, waiting for the other team to be penalized. When that happened, he'd hop over the boards on to the ice and do his thing for 90 seconds or so. Then it would be back to the bench for some more waiting.

The Canadiens' fans, who consider themselves among hockey's most knowledgeable people, began demanding Cournoyer's more frequent presence on the ice. "On Veut Cournoyer," they would scream, "On Veut Cournoyer." The translation was "We Want Cournoyer," and Coach Toe Blake didn't need a Berlitz course to get the message. He also didn't like the message.

"Why don't they let him alone?" demanded Blake. "They're putting pressure on him and they're hurting him. They're hurting the team."

The fans were certainly not trying to do that to their beloved Canadiens. They were merely hoping to encourage more use of the speedy right winger, whose heritage made him a hometown hero in Montreal. Born in Drummondville, Que., he had starred in Montreal throughout his junior hockey career, finishing with a spectacular 63 goals that led all Ontario Hockey Association shooters in his final season before graduating to the parent Canadiens.

He finished that final year of junior eligibility with a five-game trial in Montreal. He produced four goals in that brief look and had a can't miss tag hung on him for the following year. Unfortunately, he discovered that he could miss and indeed, he almost did miss. He was having trouble earning a regular job. Finally came the word that he was headed for Montreal's American League farm club at Quebec City. "It is not a demotion," insisted General Manager Sam Pollock. "He simply needs work and he can't get enough with our team."

The ticket to Quebec was a round trip one and a couple of weeks later, he was back in Montreal. This time, he stayed. "I knew then that the only place to be was with the big team. I guess I always knew that but it never occurred to me that I might not be part of it. When I got back, I said to myself, 'Yvan, this is the only place to be and you are going to work hard to be here.' Maybe it was then I started to mature."

The maturity showed during those long nights when the fans called for him and Blake left him sitting on the bench. "I will use Cournoyer on the power play or when we need a goal," he said. "He doesn't backcheck worth a damn, but some day he'll take his place as a scoring star."

As usual, Toe hit it right. Yvan scored 18 goals in his second professional season, 14 of them on the power play. In his third year, he produced 25 goals, 20 of them with Montreal enjoying a skating edge. Every so often, Blake would give him a regular turn. And slowly but surely, Cournoyer began developing into a complete hockey player.

"I loved getting those 25 goals," he said, "because I enjoy scoring more than anything else. But I was getting more work on regular shifts and that was progress."

As Cournoyer developed into a legitimate scoring threat, he began attracting considerable defensive attention, some of it legal, some of it not. While other teams stopped a step short of MacGregor's lasso idea, it sometimes seemed as though they intended trying the alternative of breaking his legs. Defensive giants hacked away at the compactly built Cournoyer like woodchoppers working on a giant oak tree.

"All they do is make me mad," said Yvan. "And when they make me mad, I play harder. Sure, they might take care of me in a fight. I'm used to that. I wish I was bigger because there are some guys I'd like to lick."

Cournoyer took the jolts but his speed helped him avoid much of the punishment. "You've got to catch him before you can belt him," noticed defenseman Brad Park of the Rangers, who did his share of the body work on the Roadrunner.

Once Cournoyer's speed got him in the clear, it was usually curtains for the other team's goalie. Yvan developed a tough, hard shot, the result of shooting steel pucks when he was a youngster. He had made the pucks himself in his father's machine shop and they paid handsome dividends.

His skill on breakaways was uncanny but Cournoyer says those are the toughest goals to score. "The more time you have to think about what you're going to do, the more things you think about and that's when you make a mistake," he explained.

So Yvan keeps the thinking to a minimum, depending instead on his hockey savvy. The technique has served him well with 316 goals in 10 seasons including four years in which he scored 40 or more. He set a playoff scoring record with 15 goals in leading Montreal to the Stanley Cup in 1973, the year he won the Conn Smythe Trophy as Most Valuable Player in the playoffs.

Now the fans no longer have to chant, "On Veut Cournoyer." They get Cournoyer regularly. He has become Montreal's most fearsome scorer. The Roadrunner has arrived.

Beep-beep.

PHIL ESPOSITO

The date was May 15, 1967. In Chicago, it lives on as a day of infamy. In Boston, it's just a day to remember happily. For that was the day that Milt Schmidt, then general manager of the Boston Bruins, sweet-talked Tommy Ivan, GM of the Black Hawks, out of Phil Esposito.

It was a three-for-three trade, and in Ivan's defense, it must be said that it didn't seem that one-sided at the time. The Bruins sent smallish center Pit Martin, defenseman Gilles Marotte and goalie Jack Norris to the Black Hawks for Esposito and two other forwards, Fred Stanfield and Ken Hodge.

Esposito had played four years in Chicago, mostly as the center for Bobby Hull. He had developed into a solid National Hockey League player, nothing extraordinary but no slouch either. His trade caused very little excitement at the time, except in Boston where solid NHL players had been in short supply.

The Bruins had been living at the bottom of the NHL for almost a decade. They had missed the playoffs for eight straight seasons and even the arrival of a marvelously gifted teen-aged defenseman named Bobby Orr had been unable to move the club up in the standings in 1966-67. The team had won just 17 games that season and finished buried in last place. Clearly, some changes were required. The first, and most important, was the installation of Esposito in a black-and-yellow Boston jersey.

In Chicago, Espo's job was to feed Hull. He was primarily a playmaker who would position the puck for hockey's most explosive shooter, and then head for the net to scoop up any rebounds that Hull's blasts might produce.

But in Boston there was no Hull to clog the spotlight. If the Bruins were to score goals, it would be Esposito who scored

The brothers Esposito oppose each other. Boston's Phil has won five scoring titles and Chicago's Tony has won or shared three Vezina Trophies as the top goalie.

them. And if the Bruins were to make any progress in the standings, it would be the sleepy-eyed center from Sault Ste. Marie, Ontario who would lead them.

Espo responded brilliantly to the challenge. In seven years since that momentous trade, he has led all NHL scorers five times. In the two years he missed the scoring crown, he finished second. He was the first NHL shooter to score more than 100 points in a single season. He holds the NHL's single season goal-scoring record with an amazing 76 in 1970-71, the same year he set the single season point mark with 152. He has averaged an incredible 56 goals, 68 assists and 124 points in his seven years in Boston, and the club has made the playoffs all seven years and won the Stanley Cup twice.

His fabulous scoring production since he arrived in Boston has thrust Esposito among the leaders in all scoring categories. His 466 goals tie him with teammate Johnny Bucyk for seventh place on the all-time scoring list. The difference is, however, that Bucyk has played 19 seasons in the NHL, eight more than Esposito. Phil's 577 assists are 11th best in NHL history, and he is No. 9 in career points with 1,043.

Ask experts and they'll tell you that Esposito is not the best skater in the game. He is, in fact, a rather lumbering skater, lacking the grace and style you would expect from a man who has become one of hockey's most proficient scoring machines. The secret to Esposito's success then is not speed. Rather, it is his strength and his ability to stay around the net where, after all, most goals are scored.

Esposito simply plants himself in the slot—that area about 15 feet from the opposing goalie—and operates from there. He scores most of his goals from that area, not on the glamorous slap shots that Hull popularized, but rather on highly efficient snap shots.

"If you watch Phil carefully," said Harry Sinden, general manager of the Bruins, "you'll see that he almost never takes his stick back more than a foot or so. It's like a chip shot in golf, except that Espo doesn't have time to line it up. He's just incredibly accurate and quick with a snap shot that usually isn't more than three or four inches off the ice. If the goalie doesn't react instantly, he's beaten."

When Esposito's goals total began ballooning, critics refused to place him in the class of hockey's great scorers—the Richards, the Howes, the Hulls and the others. They said that Esposito was a garbage man, waiting on the goalie's doorstep to scoop up his teammates' leftovers.

"I have to laugh when people say he's in front of the net too much—that he's a garbage collector when it comes to picking up points," added Sinden. "Well, if that's the case, there are lots of guys in this league who would like to be garbage collectors. And although he never gets credit for it, he's also a super playmaker."

Esposito has won the NHL scoring crown in each of the last four seasons, and the most remarkable of those titles had to be the last one, when he finished with 145 points—58 points more than the next best scoring center in the NHL. What was remarkable about it is that Esposito wasn't even supposed to be in the Bruins' lineup until sometime in December.

The previous spring, Phil had been knocked out of the playoffs when a stiff check by New York's Ron Harris tore up his knee. It was the first serious injury in his career for this bull of a hockey player and, at age 31, his recovery was expected to be slow.

For much of the next two months after being hurt, Esposito's right leg was in a cast. He can give you a clinical description of the damage Harris' tough, clean hip check had done. "The knee ligaments were shredded like a rag mop. They had rolled up from the bottom like a window blind that you pull and let go, and down a little from the top too," he said. "The surgeons rolled the ligaments back into place, put a metal staple top and bottom, plus a piece of tendon across, to hold them in place."

Esposito remained confident that he could bounce right back as the league's best scorer as soon as the cast was removed. Then he took one look at his atrophied leg and even he had to worry. "I was pretty depressed," he admitted.

Part of that depression was caused by doctors' predictions that he wouldn't be able to return to action until mid-season. When Phil heard that, he had a sharp reply. "Well, I'll tell you, Doc," he said. "I've been looking at our exhibition schedule. There's one down here for September 27th against Chicago and I'd sure like to play against my brother, Tony, in that one."

True to his word, Espo was in that game and scored a goal. "I begged the doctors to let me play," said Phil. "I just want to see what happens when I try to play hard on it. I don't want to go into the season starting from scratch and wondering what is going to happen."

What happened was that Espo was in the Bruins' lineup opening night and scored three goals, including the 400th of his NHL career. It was the start of the second most productive year in his career. His 77 assists matched his career high and his 145 points was only seven short of the record he set in 1970-71. So much for his bad knee.

There was one alteration in Espo's style because of the knee. "I've had to change my tactics," he said. "I'm moving around more. I can't stand in the slot area as much as I used to. There are a lot of guys who are starting to look like an octopus to me."

When a man becomes as outstanding a scorer as Esposito, he must expect extra defensive attention. Sometimes that attention borders on mugging and steps over the bounds of good clean hockey. A fiery player might lose his temper with all the fouling. Instead, Espo often causes the defender to go bananas. "All it takes," said Espo, "is a little old goal and a nice loud 'Ha ha.' "

Quickly, Esposito emerged again as the leader of the Bruins' high-scoring club. The injury made no difference. He was every bit as effective as he had been before his knee collided with Harris' hip.

"You don't score goals with your knees anyway," one of Phil's teammates noted. Espo would have to agree with that. Goals are the result of a combination of factors—the ability to get off a good shot, the ability to outmaneuver an opponent for the puck and the ability to ignore the grabbing, shoving and hacking that is bound to go on in front of the net.

Even though he must rank among the game's greatest goal scorers, Esposito is a fine playmaker as well. "I don't think goals all the time," he said, although you might have trouble convincing opposing netminders of that.

Esposito's philosophy is a hand-me-down from his early days in the NHL with Chicago. "I shoot a lot," he said. "Bobby Hull always said the more you shoot, the more you'll score."

Espo has proven that his old linemate certainly knew what he was talking about.

TONY ESPOSITO

He stations himself in front of the goal net, eyes peering through slits in the grotesque mask that covers his face. He positions his body, remembering the ground rules that goalies are taught from the first day they strap on a pair of leg pads. "Stick on the ice, legs together." The words are etched in the psyche of every goalie who ever lived. He remembers the rules . . .and he breaks every one.

He is Tony Esposito and he challenges the National Hockey League's best shooters night after night in the nets of the Chicago Black Hawks. He tantalizes them with a huge gap between his leg pads, violating the first rule of goaltending. He dares shooters to try and get the puck through that opening. It's a temptation too good to ignore. So they shoot for the opening, and when they do, suddenly it's gone, and Esposito has won another showdown.

Veteran hockey observers will tell you no goalie can succeed with the awkward-looking style Esposito uses. Yet three times in his five full NHL seasons, the curly-haried netminder has had his name carved on the Vezina Trophy as the best goalie.

Esposito, whose brother, Phil, has won the league scoring crown for the last four years, is an enigma. He has often expressed the torment he feels in the nets, the pressure of playing bull's-eye for the shooters of the NHL. Yet, at the same time, he wants to play and rarely takes a night off from the shooting gallery.

Tony played in 70 of Chicago's 78 regular season games last year and responded with a flashy 2.04 goals against average and 10 shutouts, to share the Vezina with Bernie Parent of Philadelphia. Only a goal by Detroit's Marcel Dionne in the waning moments of the final game prevented Esposito from winning the award by himself.

Tony Esposito turned away this shot by Boston's veteran left winger, Johnny Bucyk.

Characteristically, Esposito took the blame for the goal that cost him the Vezina. "I just blew it," he said. From his reaction, you'd think Tony was the only Black Hawk on the ice when the other team scored. He often takes the blame for goals he allows, even when the goal is the result of the mistakes of others.

Tony takes a pragmatic view of his occupation. "Look," he once said, "it's a job. That's all, just a job." But this job is different than others. The only person comparable to a hockey goaltender is the poor soul on the receiving end of a knife-thrower's act. Playing bull's-eye is not the easiest way in the world to make a buck.

"There is pressure every time you are in there," said Esposito. "That's the name of the game—pressure. It was torture for me when I was a kid in the bantams. Phil and the other kids moaned when a puck went by me, and it's still torture if one goes in now. It's a job. I have to do it. But it's tough."

Tony and brother Phil played their first hockey in Sault Ste. Marie, Ontario and then parted company temporarily before meeting again in the NHL. Phil pursued his hockey career while Tony went off to college at Michigan Tech. Tony was named to the All American collegiate hockey squad in his sophomore and junior years at Tech.

The Montreal Canadiens had placed Tony's name on their negotiating list, and after he graduated, Esposito signed with the NHL club. After one season with Vancouver of the Western League, Tony was moved up to faster company in the Central League with Houston. Then injury problems cropped up for Montreal and he was summoned to the NHL club as an emergency replacement. His first game was to be against the Boston Bruins, whose leading scorer just happened to be brother Phil.

In the afternoon before the game, Tony called Phil. "I've been called up by the Canadiens," the goalie told his brother. "I'm playing tonight."

"Well, good luck," said Phil, "and don't be too tough on the star of the family."

Tony wasn't. Phil got two goals that night. The rest of the Bruins didn't manage any. The final score was 2-2, but Tony still maintains that both of Phil's goals were lucky shots. After the game, the brothers met. "You were lucky on the first goal and lucky on the second one," said Tony. "What the heck," answered Phil, "I'm just a lucky guy."

The brothers met twice more that season. First, Tony blanked the Bruins in a 0-0 tie, and then Boston blitzed him for 50 shots and seven goals, two of them by Phil.

Eventually, Tony returned to the minors. He had played 11 games for the Canadiens and had lost only twice. Clearly, the ex-Michigan Tech All American was good enough for the NHL. But the Canadiens had a problem. He was the club's No. 3 goalie behind Rogatien Vachon and Gump Worsley, and he represented one more goalie than the Canadiens could protect in the intra-league draft. The other clubs, particularly Chicago, were acutely aware of the Montreal problem.

Tommy Ivan, general manager of the Black Hawks, had been under heavy fire for the trade that sent Phil Esposito to the Bruins. Now he was asked whom he might pick in the June, 1969 draft. "Well," he said, "I've always liked the name Esposito. If there's some one by that name available, I might just give it some thought."

Ivan carried out his threat and drafted Tony for Chicago. It was a break for both the goalie and his new club. At the time, the Black Hawks were down, having finished in last place the year before, and were hungry for fresh faces that might start a turnaround. For Tony, that meant a chance to play and, really, that's all he ever wanted. "With the Black Hawks, I knew I would get greater opportunities to play and prove to them and to myself that I was a major league goalie."

Esposito did that in a hurry. Displaying a form that purists couldn't believe, Esposito quickly developed into a first-rate goalie for Chicago. He flopped too much, he allowed too many rebounds, he looked awkward and there was, of course, that ridiculous gap between his pads created by that rule-busting stance he took in the nets. In fact, Tony seemed to do only one thing right—to keep the puck out of the net. And that, after all, is the idea.

Tony led the league with a 2.17 goals against average that first year in the NHL and set a modern record with an amazing 15 shutouts. He won both the Vezina Trophy as the top goalie and the Calder Trophy as Rookie of the Year. He has never had a goals against average of over 2.51 and has led the league's goalies in two other years. GM Ivan thinks he knows why.

"Tony anticipates those close-in shots and those rebounds," he said. "Sure, we all know what great reflexes he has, but it's much more than that. He has tremendous power of concentration and the ability to figure where the next shot is coming from."

All that comes from playing. Any goalie will tell you that

the more he plays, the better he plays. Sitting on the bench can make a netminder rusty. That has never been a problem for Esposito.

"Both Tony and I would like to see him play 78 games if he felt up to it," said Chicago Coach Billy Reay. "But that's not possible these days with the schedule, the travel and the type of hockey we have today."

With 18 teams in the NHL, the pace is quite a strain. Yet Tony showed very little wear or tear under last year's burden of 70 games.

"Tony loves to play," Reay continued. "He'll work as often as we ask him, gladly. I realize we're in a new era, but think back to the old days, which really weren't so long ago. We had a 70-game schedule then and most clubs thought one goalie was enough. It never occurred to Gump Worsley or Glenn Hall that they needed a backup man."

Esposito, then, is a goaltending throwback, a netminder who goes out, night after night, to face the barrage of pucks. He does it because that's his job. "It's no fun playing goal," he said. "The pressure is unreal."

Esposito has adjusted to the pressure. "I'm comfortable out there and I have confidence in my ability," he said. Still, he goes into the net each night chomping on the bit of fear.

"You have to be afraid," he said. "Not afraid that you'll get hurt, but afraid they're going to score on you. Every time they come down the ice with that puck, I'm afraid it's going to go in."

So far, most of them have stayed out against the goaltending Esposito brother.

ROD GILBERT

It was lying there on the ice, camouflaged by its white color that blended in with the milky color of the frozen rink. It was an ice cream lid tossed casually, unthinkingly by a spectator, who mistook the rink surface for a trash can. And it almost ended the hockey career of Rod Gilbert.

Gilbert never saw the ice cream lid, simply because he wasn't looking for it. His eye was following the puck and his legs were churning towards the corner where the frozen hunk of rubber had landed.

The year was 1961 and Gilbert was in the final stages of a sensational junior hockey career with the Guelph, Ont. Biltmores, who were, at the time, the top amateur hockey affiliate of the National League's New York Rangers. News of Gilbert's junior hockey exploits had reached New York—39 goals in the 1959-60 season and then a league-leading 54 the following year. New York was waiting for this promising young skater—but so was that ice cream lid.

As Gilbert cut his skates to turn for the puck in the corner, he hit the cardboard lid. Suddenly he skidded. He lost control of his body as his legs flew out from under him. The next thing he knew, Gilbert lay crumpled on the ice. He had crashed into the boards and as he landed, he could feel the pain throbbing in his back. Instinctively, Rod scrambled over and dug his legs into the ice to get to his feet. It was something he had done thousands of times. It was routine for him . . . for any player who had been dumped. But this time, when Gilbert made the routine move, nothing happened. "It's gone," he thought to himself, the pain screaming through his body. "My back's gone."

They carried him off the ice on a stretcher and X-rays were ordered. They showed nothing and in the tradition of the hockey player, Gilbert ignored the pain and climbed back

Rod Gilbert has achieved NHL stardom despite two severe back operations.

into uniform. He played two more games that spring in agony that would have reduced a lesser man to tears. He simply gritted his teeth and played. But it was no good. His brain sent the right messages, but his legs couldn't carry them out. And there was always the pain . . . that dull, deep pain.

The Rangers, who had such a large part of their future riding on Rod, ordered him to the Mayo Clinic for further examinations. So they handed him a train ticket and for 17 hours, Rod Gilbert and his broken back sat on a train bound for Rochester, Minn.

When Gilbert arrived at Mayo, more X-rays were taken. This time, the fracture showed up on the plates. Dr. John Sullivan asked him a blunt question.

"Do you want to play hockey again?" the surgeon asked.

"Of course I do," said Gilbert. "It's all I know. I want to play in the NHL."

"Then you'll need a spinal fusion," said the doctor. "It's a delicate operation but it's the only way."

"Then do it," said Gilbert.

The operation was performed but instead of being out of bed in two weeks, Gilbert was still flat on his back. And now, he was more scared than ever. Complications had set in. Blood clots had developed in his left leg where bone had been taken to be grafted to his back. There was ominous talk of possible amputation.

"Oh my God," thought Gilbert. "How could this thing have happened to me?"

It became obvious that Gilbert would need another operation to deal with the clots. His spirit was down to zero. No longer was it a question of playing in the NHL. It became a matter of going out of the Mayo Clinic the way he had come in—on two legs.

The second operation was a success. Gilbert's leg was saved and after eight months of recuperation, Rod returned to the ice. He could play hockey again as Dr. Sullivan had promised he would. There was only one problem. To do it, he had to wear a cumbersome brace that resembled your grandmother's favorite corset.

"It was hard to breathe," said Gilbert. "I'd get winded fast." On the bench, Rod rarely sat down between shifts. That would only tighten the brace and make him more uncomfortable.

He played that way for three seasons, establishing himself as a Ranger regular and not missing a single game over that stretch. Then, in the summer of 1965, fate caught up with Rod Gilbert for the second time.

"I was out on the lake near my parents' cottage north of Montreal," he said. "I was boating. When I was through, I tried to pull the boat up on the shore. That was when I felt the back give way."

Always extra sensitive to any back problems after the harrowing early career experience, Gilbert notified the Rangers. This time the club flew him to Manhattan for examination by the team physician, Dr. Kazuo Yanagisawa. The diagnosis was bad. The spinal fusion had broken down under the rigors of three NHL seasons. The same type of operation would have to be done again.

"I remember him saying that I didn't really need hockey," said Gilbert, recalling his conversation with the doctor. "He said there were other things that I could do with my life. I guess he wanted to let me know there would be a risk if I kept playing hockey."

Gilbert got the message.

"But I was only 25 at the time," he said. "I didn't want to quit hockey. Playing in the National Hockey League meant everything to me. It's what I dreamed of as a boy. I had tasted what life was like in the NHL and I wasn't going to quit."

So Yanagisawa operated on Gilbert midway through the 1965-66 season. The following September, Rod showed up for training camp and took his first tenuous steps on the ice. He absorbed his first body checks, waiting, almost fearing, the moment the pain would start. It never came. Yanagisawa's handiwork was holding.

Soon, Gilbert was able to discard the corset and not long after that, Coach Emile Francis assembled a line that was to write Ranger history. At left wing was rugged Vic Hadfield. The center was slick Jean Ratelle and the right wing was Rod Gilbert. They called it the GAG line, because for one glorious season, it produced almost two goals every game. That was in 1971-72 when Gilbert scored a career-high 43 goals and 97 points, fifth highest total in the league and good enough for an All Star berth. The line combined for an impressive 139 goals and 312 points—the top single season production of any line in the league and the best production ever by a Ranger trio.

The key to the line was the right winger, Gilbert. Ranger history had always featured top shooters from the right side from the club's original captain, Bill Cook, to modern star Andy Bathgate, who held the team's scoring records of 272 goals and 729 points in 13 seasons in New York. But in 1974, 10 years after Bathgate had been traded, his scoring records fell. The guy who broke them was another right winger who was playing with a patched-up back.

Bathgate's goal record fell first. Gilbert passed that one in November with what he described as "a routine goal," against the New York Islanders. "It's a special puck for me though," he said, fingering the souvenir of his 273rd career NHL score.

Three months later, Gilbert cracked Bathgate's point mark with a pair of goals against Minnesota, raising his career total to 730 points. "Records are meant to be broken," said Rod. "Andy was my idol. I still respect his record; he did it in a different era. Like Babe Ruth and Henry Aaron."

Before the season was through, Gilbert increased his totals to 305 goals and 754 points. And after the last goal was scored and the last bodycheck absorbed, Gilbert broke the hearts of countless female Ranger fans by marching off to the altar, ending one of sport's most noted bachelorhoods.

At the time of his wedding to stewardess Judy Preston, one of National Airlines' "Fly Me" girls, Gilbert considered his career. There were more than 300 goals, more than 750 points, Ranger scoring records in both departments, a handsome six-figure salary and a beautiful bride.

"You know," he said, "that's pretty good for a guy who went under the knife 13 years ago and didn't know whether he'd wake up with part of him missing."

BOBBY HULL

His once plush, thick blond hair has thinned and the legs that once propelled him up and down the ice at lightning speeds have lost perhaps a step or two. Bobby Hull is paying the price of reaching hockey's twilight years. But make no mistake about it. There is absolutely no tarnish on the Golden Jet.

For the seventh time in his 17-year professional career, Hull hit hockey's magic 50-goal plateau last season. He finished with 53 goals and 95 points, fourth best among World Hockey Association scorers. That doesn't exactly sound like a guy ready for the hockey scrap heap.

Still, Hull must recognize the fact that there were 35 candles on his last birthday cake and those are nervous numbers for hockey players. But then Hull's recent career has been intermingled with numbers—numbers like $1,000,000, the up-front figure he got when he jumped from the National Hockey League to the new WHA.

There are very few players who could give a new league like the WHA instant respectability. Hull was one of them and so the WHA went after him. The logical franchise was Winnipeg, which offered Bobby a chance to return his family to the rural surroundings he missed in Chicago. Ben Hatskin, owner of the Jets, convinced the other WHA clubs that it would be in their best interests to help him piece together a package that would lure Hull to the new league.

The first contact between Hatskin and Hull came in a Vancouver hotel lobby. "He told me, 'I'm gonna get you,' " recalled Hull of the conversation between owner and player.

Hatskin knew that Bobby would listen to an offer. Hull had played 15 years in Chicago, but the last few had been tempered by bad feelings between the player and his club.

Seven times in 17 seasons of professional hockey, Bobby Hull of Winnipeg has scored 50 goals or more.

The disputes were over little things—embarrassments that a 50-goal scorer shouldn't have to endure. Hull was hassled because he brought his youngsters to a practice. He was ordered to make a public apology after a holdout. He was ordered to change his exciting offensive style, to become more of a team player.

When the WHA opened for business, Hull wasn't knocking down any doors or leading the dash from the established

NHL. Instead, the new league went looking for Hull. And each time Hatskin's lawyers talked with Hull's, the negotiations became more serious.

Finally, Chicago saw fit to jump into the conversations, making Hull an offer of its own. Harvey Weinberg, Hull's chief negotiator, reported the counter offer, calling it "very good," but said it "couldn't come close to the WHA offer."

Even Hull had to be impressed. "I'm 33," he said during the bidding. "At that age, I'm gratified that I should be offered so much for playing a game."

Soon the negotiating was reaching the nitty gritty stage. "I was going to sign a five-year contract with Chicago," admitted Hull. But Hatskin wouldn't give up. He just hiked the numbers a little more. "It got to the point," said Bobby, "where I couldn't say no to Ben."

And so, he said yes. It was a yes that set the NHL back on its heels. There had been 33 WHA jumpers before Hull, but lumped together, they hardly measured up to the prestige, talent and charisma that the WHA had achieved with the Hull coup. Here was one of hockey's best players, only the second man in history to score 600 goals, the only player ever to achieve 13 consecutive 30-or-more goal seasons, five 50-goal seasons. He had led the NHL in goals seven times and in scoring three times. He had won the Hart Trophy as most valuable player twice. He was a giant of the game and here he was, turning his back on the established NHL and crossing over to the new kid on hockey's big league block.

The lure that caught Hull was a 10-year $2.75 million contract that included that fantastic $1 million up front. When he signed his contract, he was rewarded with a giant-sized check and flashed a million-dollar grin as he posed with it alongside his wife. "You have made this the most memorable day of our lives," he told WHA officials at the signing. "I'm very gratified."

The deal called for Hull to perform double duty as player and coach for the Winnipeg Jets and there is a suspicion that his role as bench boss was also a major factor in his move to the WHA. For the first time, Hull had a hand in the running of his team.

"For 15 years with the Black Hawks, I just followed instructions and the schedule without thinking about it," said Hull. "I came to training camp the same time every year. I played with the same guys and largely under the same coach, went to the same buildings in the same towns and lived in the same city, Chicago," he said.

"Now, all of a sudden, I've come into a new atmosphere. I've turned my life completely around. I'm no longer following the crowd. I'm playing in different cities, with different players, meeting new people, living in a town that's new to me, working under different conditions."

The success of the Jets and the WHA became a personal challenge for Hull. He drove himself without let-up. In every town he visited, appearances were arranged. After games, he'd linger until the last autograph was signed. He was selling the WHA now and doing a pretty good job of it.

The NHL reacted to Hull's jump in a rather vindictive fashion. First it barred him from playing for Team Canada in the series against the Russian National team. It was almost as if he had lost his citizenship by crossing league lines. Then the Black Hawks went to court and succeeded in throwing legal roadblocks that kept him off the ice for Winnipeg's first 15 games.

"It was a difficult period for me," said Hull, "both mentally and physically. I wanted to play and I couldn't. And it was impossible to stay in shape without game conditions."

Finally, Bobby got the green light to resume game action and even though he missed all those early games, he still finished with 51 goals and 103 points, the fourth best figure in the league. What's more, he coached Winnipeg to first place in the West Division and into the finals of the playoffs for the World Cup.

What kind of a coach was Hull in his first year? The answer comes from some of his players.

"Bobby's preaching to us what he has done himself," said

Chris Bordeleau. "Everyone respects his knowledge of the game."

"He takes his job as coach seriously," said Milt Black. "He leads by showing."

"It's terrific having him on the same team," offered goalie Joe Daley. "Do I envy the money he's making? No way! He's worth every cent. He's a great hockey player and a great guy."

In his second season as coach of the Jets, Hull noticed some disturbing traits, not only among his own players but among younger hockey players in general. It was called a lack of dedication and discipline. And when Hull complained about it, ex-teammate Lou Angotti used Bobby's remarks to launch a long-range shot at Hull.

Angotti, who had at least as much hockey talent in his whole body as Hull has in his left forearm, blasted Bobby. "He doesn't have it (discipline from his team) as a coach because he didn't have it as a player. He could miss practice. He could fly out of town on business. He never sat down and looked at Lou Angotti or Chico Maki and said, 'These guys aren't getting the same privileges as me.' How about all the times we were ordered to get on the bus right after a game, only to have to wait for him to sign autographs?"

It's funny, but Angotti never complained about those irritations when Hull was scoring all those goals for the Black Hawks and helping put playoff checks in the pockets of his terribly inconvenienced and underprivileged teammates.

What Angotti forgot to mention was that Hull earned everything he's ever had in hockey on the ice as one of the game's greatest players. He has been the sport's No. 1 goodwill ambassador and after selling the NHL for the better part of 15 seasons, he's now doing the same thing for the WHA. Ben Hatskin wouldn't have it any other way.

RICK MARTIN

Contrary to popular belief, hockey general managers do not spend all of their time concerned with the records of their current teams. The future occupies a great deal of their time, and probably the most important part of the future in hockey is the amateur draft. That is the time of year when the big league teams divide up Canada's most promising junior hockey players—a key time to build for the future.

Before the draft, there is always a lot of jockeying. Teams try to anticipate who will finish with the poorer records and thus have the earliest picks at the new junior crop. Then the trick is to arrange a trade with one of those clubs so that their draft choice will go to you. It's a guessing game, but sometimes it can pay off handsomely.

The 1971 amateur draft showcased a particularly fertile class of graduating juniors. The No. 1 choice belonged to Montreal, not because the Canadiens had the worst record, but because GM Sammy Pollock had arranged a trade earlier with the California club. It was a foregone conclusion that Pollock would choose everybody's candidate for top choice, right wing Guy Lafleur. Detroit owned the No. 2 choice and Buffalo GM Punch Imlach suggested a trade. The Sabres wanted that No. 2 selection so that they could pick Marcel Dionne, who had starred at St. Catherine's, just across the border from Buffalo. Detroit turned down the proposal, though, and Dionne wound up with the Red Wings. After two more players were picked—defenseman Jocelyn Guvremont by Vancouver and center Gene Carr by St. Louis—Imlach had his pick. The Sabres' section was left wing Rick Martin, whose credentials included a league-leading 71 goals for Montreal in his final season in the Ontario Hockey Association.

It didn't take Imlach long to realize that he had drafted a

Rick Martin (7) became a 50-goal scorer in his third NHL season.

superstar. In his first season with the Sabres, Martin produced 44 goals—a record for rookies in the NHL. Tick off the names of hockey's greatest scorers—Hull, Howe, Richard, Beliveau—none of them scored as many goals in their first seasons as Martin did in his.

"Martin is the best goal scorer I've ever coached," declared Imlach, who has had clubs with such renowned shooters as Beliveau and Frank Mahovlich on them.

"This kid is one of those players with special gifts," continued Imlach. "He has those little skills for producing goals that only very few players have.

"He doesn't have the stamina of a Mahovlich or a Beliveau, but he can score goals more ways. He can overpower goalies with his slap shot, hit with his wrist shot or his great backhand and, in close traffic, he just has that touch for doing the right thing."

Martin was no flash in the pan. Following that 44-goal first year, he scored 37 in 1972-73 and then joined hockey's 50-goal club with 52 last year, including three in the final game of the season to go over the plateau. That's 133 goals in three seasons, the kind of production that makes Imlach happy about Buffalo's future. Sometimes Punch remembers how close he came to the trade with Detroit, and choosing Dionne instead of Martin. "It just shows you," the Sabres' boss philosophized, "that everything turns out for the best."

Martin's success in the NHL is no accidental thing. He works long and hard at the game of hockey and is usually the last Sabre player off the ice at practice. He is a tireless skater who works diligently at his shots—the booming slapper and the quick, accurate wrist.

"I depend on the wrist shot 75% of the time," he said. "I use the slap shot only from the blue line, when there's a lot of traffic in front of the net. The wrist shot is more accurate and you have a quickness edge on the goalie, who hasn't as much of a chance to get set."

That shows a certain maturity about this handsome 23-year-old who grew up in the suburbs of Montreal. He wasn't always so stuck on the wrist shot. There was a time when the more glamorous slapper was his main weapon.

"Bobby Hull had brought in the slap shot when I was just a baby—around eight—and it really caught on. I can remember breaking five or six sticks a week practicing it. My father really chewed me out for that. It was shooting, shooting, shooting. And it paid off."

That was fine when Martin was a teen-ager burning up

midget and juvenile leagues. "I knew I could make it as a hockey pro when I was 13," he said. "I was playing in both the bantam and the midget leagues then, and I was top scorer in both of them, 85 goals in the bantams and 30 in the midgets." In amateur hockey, Martin played for the Junior Canadiens. His center was Gilbert Perreault, whom Imlach had drafted a year before selecting Rick in the junior draft. The reunion has helped both players. "I know where he goes," said Martin. "I know what he's going to do so I can anticipate where I should go. And he knows my game, too, so it works both ways."

Martin found out fast that he needed more than that booming slapper to succeed in the big league surroundings of the NHL. "I certainly figured it would be harder to play here than in the juniors, and it certainly is," he said. "The defense is better and the forwards check a lot harder in the NHL. You have somebody checking you all the time. And the goalies don't give you much to shoot at. You have to shoot faster and let it go farther out."

The need to shoot faster was a main factor in Rick's move to the wrist shot. "The slap shot lets me get set up and I'm more accurate with it. But I'm faster getting off the wrist shot," he said.

The game of hockey moves with such speed that most of the offensive plays are innovated on the spot as responses to situations in which the skaters find themselves. There would seem to be very little room for planning. There just isn't time. Yet, Martin has reduced his movement to stop-action. He can describe the action step by step, from the time he gets the puck on his stick to the moment he launches his shot.

"I try to stick to positional hockey," he said. "I stay on my wing, but once I get across the blue line, I try to go into the goal on a straight line. That way, I have balance for shooting. I always try to aim for a spot. But the trick is to stick with your decision about the spot."

Martin's eyes light up when he discusses his job. "Shooting is just plain fun. You're carrying the puck, feeling it move from the tip to the heel [of the stick] and you make your move. You look at the net—you can see the mesh behind the guy's body. Where the goalie's not, that's where you want to shoot. Then you look back down at the puck to just double-check where it is. Then you shoot, and you watch the puck through its trajectory. Just before it reaches the guy, you know if it's in. If the goalie made the first move, you've usually got him. If he stayed tough, it's up to you to make the opening. It's harder to beat the guy who doesn't move. Anyway, you've just got to keep moving in for the rebound, because you never know if there won't be one."

When he joined the Sabres, Martin moved right in with Perreault, his old friend from junior hockey. That gave Imlach a left wing and a center. All the line lacked was a right wing and Imlach got that man when Buffalo acquired Rene Robert. The trio was tabbed the French Connection—all three have Quebec heritage—and it has become one of the most prolific lines in the league.

The arrival of Martin helped build Buffalo into one of the NHL's better expansion teams. The accent is on youth and the young Sabres have developed into an impressive club. Most of the improvement can be traced to Perreault and Martin. Even the Sabres' older players have been impressed.

"All I know," said goalie Roger Crozier, one of the team's graybeards, "is I hope I'm still around when those two lead us out of the wilderness."

And every time some ambitious general manager approaches Punch Imlach with a proposal about his amateur draft selections, the Sabres' GM just smiles and shakes his head. He'll stick with his own draft turns, thank you. They have served him well so far.

BOBBY ORR

The beauty of sports can be captured in the performances of individual competitors. The essence of basketball is Julius Erving, driving for the basket, soaring high in the air and then driving the ball through the hoop. In baseball, it's Hank Aaron, setting himself in the batter's box, then swinging his body into a pitch, snapping his wrists and sending the ball on its way for another home run. In football, it's O. J. Simpson, following his blockers into the line and then bursting through the narrowest opening to churn out the yards.

Hockey's art and grace, its power and strength, are also all wrapped up in one performer. He's Bobby Orr of the Boston Bruins, easily one of the game's most dynamic players. When Orr gathers in a loose puck behind his own net and then starts out, skating easily, cradling the puck on the blade of his stick, the roar, like Orr's speed, begins slowly. Then, as Bobby gets to the center red line, he really starts moving. By the time he reaches the attacking zone the crowd is howling and Orr is moving like a locomotive with the next stop being the other team's net.

"He is like a gear-shift car," observed Ted Green, an old Boston teammate of Bobby's. "He's got 15 speeds of fast."

Orr rushing the puck is what hockey's all about. He is smooth and graceful, despite a gimpy left knee that has been operated on three times and may eventually force an early end to one of hockey's most spectacular careers.

There have been outstanding defensemen before, belters such as Boston's Eddie Shore and finesse specialists such as Montreal's Doug Harvey and Detroit's Red Kelly. But never has any defenseman changed the complexion of this game the way the baby-faced kid from Parry Sound, Ont. did when he arrived in the NHL.

Orr was only 18 years old when he came to Boston in

Boston's Bobby Orr captured the Norris Trophy as the NHL's best defenseman for the seventh straight season in 1973-74.

1966-67 and his play was obviously rough around the edges. But hockey's pros could see even then that this young man was going to be something special.

The James Norris Trophy, awarded to the NHL's best defenseman that season, went to veteran Harry Howell of the New York Rangers. Howell, always a gentleman, grinned from ear to ear when he accepted his trophy at the league's award luncheon. "I'm glad I won this thing this year," said Howell, "because I have a feeling that from now on, it's going to belong to Bobby Orr."

Howell made that statement seven years ago and, so far, his prediction has been perfect. Orr has won the Norris seven straight times and that accomplishment alone would earn him considerable recognition among the league's defensemen. He has, however, accomplished much more.

Three times, Orr has been voted the league's Most Valuable Player. Shore, with four, is the only defenseman to have earned that honor more than Bobby.

Until Orr came along, only one defenseman in history had scored 20 goals in a season. Orr has scored 20 or more in each of the last six seasons.

Until Orr came along, no defenseman had ever led his team in scoring. In 1969-70, Orr had not only led the Bruins but the rest of the league as well with an incredible 120 points. He became the first defenseman to win the Art Ross Trophy as the scoring champion. As impressive as that point total was, Orr surpassed it the next season with 139, including an unbelievable 102 assists, another record. The only reason he didn't win the scoring crown that year was that teammate Phil Esposito picked the same season to score his record of 152 points. In fact, Orr has finished second in the scoring race to Esposito three times and third once—remarkable accomplishments for a defenseman.

But Orr is not a defenseman in the traditional style of a Shore or a Harvey or a Kelly. Bobby has revolutionized the position he plays. He has made the defenseman an attacker who, if he can skate like Orr, can be every bit as dangerous offensively as a center or a winger.

To go with his MVP, best defenseman and scoring champion hardware, Orr's mantelpiece also includes the Calder Trophy as Rookie of the Year in 1966-1967 and two Conn Smythe Trophies as playoff MVP. In 1969-70, the Bruins won their first Stanley Cup in 29 years, and the man who scored the Cup-winning goal in overtime was Bobby Orr.

The next year, Orr began reaping a healthy cash return from his talent. He had come into pro hockey when the game's salaries were still in the dark ages of sport. But he demanded and got a healthy contract to turn pro. When it ran out, his attorney launched negotiations with the Bruins for a new one and it took 18 months to finalize the details. Those details included some fancy numbers—something like $1 million for five years. The negotiating was done by attorney Alan Eagleson, who had first met Orr a decade before in Bobby's home town of Parry Sound.

"Today," said Eagleson at the signing ceremony, "he is exactly the same person I first met 10 years ago, even though there is no doubt now that he is one of the world's greatest athletes."

His current five-year contract carries Orr through 1976 and there are some indications that it could be the last one he signs with the Bruins. There are two factors here. One is his left knee and the other is Orr himself. Bobby realizes there are other things in this world besides hockey.

"I'll be a 10-year man then [in 1976] and I think I'd welcome at least a year off to travel somewhere—maybe to Ireland where my grandfather came from—and just relax and do what I like," he said after signing his current contract.

"But that's a 23-year-old kid talking. Maybe, by 1976, I'll be so gung-ho about hockey I wouldn't dream of something like that."

Then, there is the matter of his knee. He had cartilage removed from it during the 1967-68 season, reinjured it the next year and then had another operation in 1972. He was scheduled for the third operation well in advance of the end of the 1972 season and was performing in the playoffs under a severe handicap. Still, he led the Bruins to another Stanley Cup and again was named the tournament's Most Valuable Player. "He was better on one leg," admired Emile Francis, general manager-coach of the New York Rangers, "than anybody else was on two."

Dr. Jerry Wilson, a Winnipeg orthopedic physician and a former hockey player himself who had knee problems very similar to Orr's, predicted that the Boston star would only play a few more years.

"I would say he could play five or six years," said Dr. Wilson, "but I predict he wouldn't probably play more than a couple because his ability will go and he won't be able to tolerate that very long. He'll be an ordinary hockey player."

Dr. Wilson said the description used by Orr's surgeon—"osteophyte pinching the nerve,"—could be the tip-off. "An osteophyte is a term used for degenerative arthritis," said Dr. Wilson. "So this is how I assume that he must have had arthritis, of a moderately severe degree, in there and this is a condition that does not get better in time. It just gets worse with more trauma, more work on it."

Although Orr would be the last one to question a physician's professional opinion, it should be pointed out that since Bobby's knee was last opened for surgery, he has played two seasons and shown absolutely no signs of slipping from his pedestal as one of the game's finest players.

Milt Schmidt, longtime general manager of the Bruins and now GM of the NHL's new Washington Capitals, probably summed up Orr best.

"In all my years in hockey," said Schmidt, "Bobby is the greatest player I have ever seen in the past, the greatest of the present, and if anybody better should ever come along, I just hope the Good Lord keeps me around here so I can see him."

Another way of judging the NHL's Age of Orr is the one Harry Sinden, Boston's current GM, uses. Sinden was Orr's coach when Bobby broke into the NHL and is often asked when he first realized that this blond youngster was going to be a star.

"Bobby Orr became a star in the NHL," Sinden likes to say, "about the time they played the National Anthem for his first game with us."

Sinden hasn't had any argument with that observation so far.

BERNIE PARENT

Masks have been a source of annoyance for many goaltenders. Sure, they have become vital tools of the trade in the slap shot-happy world of hockey where a puck can change direction faster than you can say Jacques Plante. And, of course, almost every goalie has accepted the face protector. But that doesn't mean they have to like that hunk of fibreglass enveloping their profiles.

So most goalies strap on their masks only when it is absolutely necessary. In a pre-game skate, they lope around the ice with the mask stuffed in their leg pads or lying idly atop the goal net. When the National Anthem is played, they stand bare-faced. Only when the action starts does the mask go on. Many will take it off during play stoppages, and almost all will do it as soon as the period or game ends.

There is one glaring exception to that practice. In Philadelphia, goalie Bernie Parent appears on the ice for the pre-game warmup with his mask securely in place. He leaves the ice the same way, at the end of each period and after every game. On the ice, no one sees Parent's face.

A writer asked Bernie about it one day and the goalie had a straight-forward reply. "I will take off my mask," Parent said mysteriously, "the day we win the Stanley Cup."

And Parent stuck to his word. As soon as the last second had ticked off, finishing Boston in the sixth game of the championship series and delivering the Cup to the Cinderella Flyers, Parent tore off that mask, revealing his face for the first time all season on the ice. The losing Bruins were relieved to see Parent's profile. For awhile, they thought that a machine was guarding the Flyer goal.

Midway through last season when it became obvious that the Flyers were on their way to a year to remember, a bumper sticker began appearing around town. "Only the Lord saves

Philadelphia goalie Bernie Parent shared the Vezina Trophy and won the Conn Smythe Trophy as playoff MVP last year.

more than Bernie Parent,'' it said. No blasphemy was intended. The fact was that the well-traveled goalie enjoyed one heavenly season.

The year started with a 2-0 shutout of his ex-teammates, the Toronto Maple Leafs, and it ended with a 1-0 shutout that clinched the Cup against his first NHL team, the Boston Bruins. And after he finished with a shutout that which he had started with a shutout, Parent grinned and said, ''This is where I came in.''

There were 93 games in between those shutouts and Parent played in 88 of them. He missed five games somewhere along the line and if they let him, he'll make up for that little oversight this year. In the era of the two and three-goalie system, Parent was an iron man, strapping on the 40 pounds or so of pads to face the barrage of enemy shots night after night. He not only was the most durable goalie in the league but he was the best one too. He turned in 12 regular season shutouts and a 1.89 goals against average, then added two more shutouts during the playoffs, nailing down the Conn Smythe Trophy as the Stanley Cup tournament's Most Valuable Player.

When the last second had ticked off for the Bruins, Parent expressed his joy, ripping off his mask to celebrate. It is traditional for the captain of the winning Cup team to accept the trophy on behalf of his teammates and circle the ice, toting the silverware for all to admire. Bobby Clarke, captain of the Flyers, carried out his job, but he had company. Parent was right there with his teammate, helping him lug the Cup. And no Flyer deserved a piece of that action more than the gutsy goalie.

"Don't write about us winning the Stanley Cup," Clarke advised the writers in the slightly soggy Philly dressing room later. "Write about Bernie. He won it."

Indeed, Parent deserved a lion's share of the credit for giving Philadelphia its first winner in what seemed like centuries. He had been like the Great Wall of China in front of the Flyer net, blocking just about everything shot his way. It was as if Philadelphia's lucky charm, ample Kate Smith, had parked herself and her piano as well in the goal mouth.

Parent played like a man possessed. And he was possessed—possessed with the dream of winning the Stanley Cup. "You are maybe five or six years old, growing up in Canada, when you first realize the importance of winning the Stanley Cup," the goalie explained. "I watched a game in Montreal when I was a boy, Canadiens against Chicago, and they played and played until it was almost two o'clock in the morning. Such a tremendous thing. I wondered to myself, 'I wonder what the feeling must be to play for the Cup.' "

Now Bernie knows and when the prize was finally nailed down, he wanted to be a part of that beautiful moment. "I thought back to those times as a kid, watching other guys circle the ice with the Cup," he said. "Then I thought of the hundreds and thousands of hockey players who will never get this opportunity. Even if you had a hundred million dollars, you couldn't buy the feeling we have now."

The Flyers had paid the down payment for the feeling 11 months before when they acquired the rights to Parent from Toronto. The Maple Leafs weren't too hesitant about surrendering those rights though, because Parent's most recent address at the time had been the World Hockey Association.

Now if that sounds a little confusing, it's all right. Parent's road to the Stanley Cup took a few strange turns. It started in Boston in the days when the Bruins were a rather downtrodden team. He was a promising goalie and when he was made available in the 1967 expansion draft, he was the first player chosen by Philadelphia.

Bernie played 3½ productive seasons for the Flyers before General Manager Keith Allen's fancy was whetted by a good looking young forward in the Boston organization. The result was a three-way trade with Toronto getting Parent for Mike Walton and the Flyers shipping Walton to Boston for two prospects, one of them Rick MacLeish. They could never have guessed it at the time but Parent and MacLeish, the key men in this trade, would be sipping Stanley Cup champagne together three years later.

At Toronto, Parent was teamed with his goaltending idol, Jacques Plante. Learning at the master's knee, he began developing into a young Plante. He even adopted Jacques' specially-designed mask and acquired many of the old goalie's tricks, like skating to his bench for "equipment repairs" to short circuit the opposition's momentum.

The Parent-Plante combine operated for 2½ seasons but Bernie had a problem. His bride wasn't thrilled with the Canadian winters and when the WHA came along with a franchise in, of all places, Miami, Carol Parent had a little talk with her goaltender husband. Then Carol Parent's goaltender husband had a talk with his lawyer. And soon, the WHA had its first jumper. Parent posed proudly with the jersey of the marvelously named Miami Screaming Eagles.

Despite that spectacular nickname, Miami's WHA franchise never got off the ground, primarily because of the absence of an ice arena in which to play. Undaunted, the WHA moved the franchise to Philadelphia, which was just fine with Carol and Bernie since Mrs. Parent came from nearby Cherry Hill, N.J.

Parent began his first season in the WHA with the Philadelphia Blazers wearing uniform No. 00, quite appropriate for a goalie but about a year early for Parent. In the wide-open offensive world of the WHA, Parent struggled under the burden of a 3.61 average. He suffered a broken foot that cost him a fistful of games but when he returned, he played 55 straight games. When the streak reached 50, Bernie revealed that he was having frequent talks with his brother, who is a psychiatrist. When it was suggested that the pressure must be getting to him, Bernie laughed. "Actually," the goalie said, "he calls me. You know, you can go bananas in that job."

When the playoffs arrived, a contract dispute surfaced and Parent's consecutive game streak ended abruptly. The split between goalie and the Blazers couldn't be mended and Parent began looking back over his shoulder at the NHL. Not in the direction of Toronto, which still owned his rights, but to Philadelphia. After all, Carol Parent liked the neighborhood.

A deal was arranged and GM Keith Allen proudly announced Parent's return. "We are extremely happy to have Bernie back with us," Allen said. "We consider him one of the top goalies in hockey and anytime you have a chance to obtain a player of his calibre, you jump at it.

"Trading Bernie away was the toughest thing I've ever had to do in hockey. Bringing him back is one of the most pleasant."

Parent's play made the season the most pleasant any expansion team has ever had. He led the Flyers to the West Division title, shared the Vezina Trophy as the top goalie, and then carried the club to the Cup. And the man who scored the winning goal—in fact the only goal—in that sixth game clincher, was, ironically, Rich MacLeish, the man for whom the Flyers had once traded away Bernie Parent.

BRAD PARK

The telephone rang in Brad Park's Manhattan hotel a couple of hours before Park and the New York Rangers were to take the ice against the Boston Bruins. It was a Friday night, usually a night off for the Rangers. But on this particular evening, the Rangers and Bruins had a date in Madison Square Garden. It was to be the start of the National Hockey League's televised Game of the Week series, and in an effort to get the series off on the right foot, two of the best clubs were matched for the first show. As a result, Park was alone in a Manhattan hotel room instead of with his wife, at home in Long Beach expecting their second child in a couple of months.

Park picked up the phone. There was a note of urgency in the voice at the other end. A neighbor was calling to tell Brad that his wife was on the way to the hospital.

Immediately, Park called his boss, general manager Emile Francis. "Get over there," said Francis. "Don't worry about the game."

Park rushed to the Long Island Railroad and caught a train. When he got to the Manhasset stop in the midst of the rush hour, there were no cabs in sight. Then a Ranger fan recognized the All Star defenseman and asked if he needed help. "I sure do," said Park. "My wife's giving birth at North Shore Hospital."

"Relax," said the fan. "My wife is a nurse there. She'll be fine." With that, the fan drove Park to the hospital in time to welcome his new son, Robbie, into the world. Then the fan chauffeured the slightly shook father to the Garden for the game with the Bruins.

Brad arrived too late for the pre-game warmup, but he missed only the game's first shift. When he arrived on the bench, the alert Garden crowd noticed his presence im-

Brad Park (2) was the Rangers' leading scorer last season.

mediately, and, unaware of the pre-game drama, cheered. Not long after, Park hit the ice and gave his newborn son a birthday present—a goal.

It was a memorable night for Park, and little Robbie was to be the impetus for a more harrowing one just a couple of months later. The tiny baby contracted viral pneumonia and doctors expressed fear that they would lose him. He was so tiny, so helpless, up against rather tough odds. The doctors told Park and his wife, Gerri, not to be too hopeful when they returned Robbie to the hospital.

"It's out of our hands," said Brad, his face showing the tension of a helpless father, waiting for the fate of his child to be determined. "The doctors say the next 36 hours are crucial." Park bit his lip. What could he do? His hands were tied. He could only wait, confident that the doctors would do their best to save his small son's life.

That night the Rangers played the California Seals and Brad Park, with his mind a million miles away, scored two goals. It was as if he was trying to help his son, some way, any way. He played a superb game, and after it was over, he rushed to his wife's side to resume the vigil.

Little Robbie Park made it through that crisis. Somehow, his tiny body fought off the infection, and when his son recovered, Brad stood in the Ranger dressing room to thank the teammates who had tried to help him through the toughest crisis a parent can face.

His teammates rallied around Park for two basic reasons. First, it was the humane thing to do. Second, Brad Park is the heart and soul of their hockey club. He is the leader of their team—the man who plays the key role in their performance, offensively and defensively.

Brad Park wears uniform No. 2 and in a way it is symbolic. If he had come into the NHL at any other time in history, he undoubtedly would be considered the game's most dominant defenseman because of his enormous talent. It was, however, Park's poor fortune to come along at approximately the same time as Boston's Bobby Orr, and you don't have to be a hockey expert to know that Orr is the best defenseman in the history of the game.

Park laughs at the irony of his situation. "I don't mind being number two," he has said. "I'll try harder."

Park's development into a superstar is one reason NHL teams try harder each June in the NHL's various drafts.

That's because the Rangers picked Park up in one of those drafts back in 1966. Brad had played his junior hockey for the Toronto Marlboros, a Maple Leafs' club, but an administrative slipup made him available for the draft. New York grabbed him and King Clancy, a hockey Hall of Famer and assistant general manager of the Maple Leafs, still bemoans the blunder. "I don't know how it happened," he said. "I don't know how we let him get away."

After that draft, Park had two more years of junior hockey at Toronto, but as property of the Rangers, carefully protected against being accidentally lost in any drafts. In 1968 he turned 20 and showed up for his first NHL training camp. He had an abundance of two vital commodities—talent and confidence. He took one look around camp and boldly declared that he'd make this team. He almost did, too. He was the last player cut, and there are those who will tell you that he never should have been dropped. But the Rangers were more or less committed to big Al Hamilton, who had two years of minor league experience and was waiting for his first shot at the NHL.

Park was shipped out to the American League, a demotion that lasted only 17 games. He averaged nearly a point per game in the AHL, and as soon as the opportunity arose, he was summoned back to New York. This time, he stayed.

He quickly moved into the starting lineup and it became obvious that he was a promising young talent. As the Rangers' faith in the young man increased, so did his contributions to their game. Soon he was being given the important assignment of rushing the puck out of New York's end of the ice—lugging the puck into the offensive zone to set up the play. He was becoming the quarterback of the Ranger attack.

"He is like a fourth forward out there," admired Francis. "He gives us the most mobile defense in the league."

The Ranger forwards all appreciated Park's ability to rush the puck. "With him controlling the puck," said Rod Gilbert, "it gives us a chance to get into the open. When we do, he makes the play. He always thinks far ahead of the play and that results in more scoring opportunities.''

His style in the offensive zone reminded everybody of a talented defenseman who plays in Boston. ''Park is the Rangers' Orr,'' said Milt Schmidt, former general manager of the Bruins and now GM of the new Washington Capitals. ''He is vital in three areas—running the offense, working the power play from the point and killing penalties.''

Orr has won the Norris Trophy as the NHL's best defenseman seven straight seasons. Park has been runner-up in that balloting three of those years. For half a century, the only NHL defenseman to score 20 goals in a season was an obscure fellow named Flash Hollett, who did it for Detroit in 1944-45. The second man to do it was Bobby Orr. The only other defensive player to score 20 goals was Park. Orr became the first defenseman ever to lead his team in scoring. Two others have accomplished the feat since the Boston star turned the trick. One of them was Park.

In their personal game of ''Anything You Can Do, I Can Do Better,'' Orr always seems to get there first. But once, Park set the standard. That was in 1971-72 when Brad became the first defenseman in history to score the hat trick—three goals in one game—twice in the same season. Strangely, the victim on both nights was goalie Jim Rutherford, who would be first on line to testify to Park's offensive abilities.

Ask Park about the Orr syndrome and he just grins. ''I'm me and he's him.'' he says. ''He plays his game and I play mine.''

DENIS POTVIN

From the bright hope of training camp in Peterborough, Ontario to the jitters of opening night in Atlanta, to exciting home-ice victories over the New York Rangers and Boston Bruins, to a dismal mid-season slump and the eventual realization that they were doomed to another last-place finish, the New York Islanders rode an emotional season-long seesaw.

Now there was only one game left—a meaningless last-night stand against the Minnesota North Stars, a club, like New York, struggling to a dismal finish. Given the circumstances, you could understand if the North Star and Islander players might not be up to putting on a classical hockey display. Neither team had much incentive.

But for one player, there was plenty of incentive. As he placed his helmet squarely on his head in the Islander dressing room, rookie defenseman Denis Potvin thought of the job he faced. "Two points," thought Potvin. "I've got to get those two points."

Potvin went into that final game with a season total of 50 points, one less than the NHL single-season record for a rookie defenseman, set by Vancouver's Jocelyn Guevremont in 1971-72. One more point would tie Guevremont and two would put Potvin in the record book, no small achievement for a young man playing with the often-hapless Islanders.

The Islanders scored four goals in that final game. Potvin assisted on the first two, breaking Guevremont's record, celebrated his accomplishment with his 17th goal of the season, and then capped off a perfect night with another assist on New York's final goal.

Potvin finished the season with 17 goals and 54 points, both rookie records, and led the Islanders in scoring, becoming only the third defenseman in NHL history to finish the

Defenseman Denis Potvin (5) led the New York Islanders in scoring and was the NHL's Rookie of the Year last season.

year as his team's best scorer. The other two were Boston's Bobby Orr and Brad Park of the Rangers, pretty fast company for any defenseman, particularly a rookie.

Orr . . . there's that name again. It's the one Potvin heard repeated over and over again throughout his outstanding junior career with the Ottawa 67s. The parallels were hard to overlook. Both had been teen-aged hockey prodigies, defensemen who played the game with a poise that belied their years. Orr established junior hockey scoring records for defensemen and Potvin smashed them. Inevitably, Denis was described as "the next Orr." He preferred, however, to be the next Potvin, following his older but less talented brother, Jean, into the NHL.

"I hope people soon forget about the Orr thing," said Potvin. "I'm not an Orr and neither is anybody else. I just want to be Denis Potvin, a good NHL defenseman."

Good rookie defensemen sign for healthy bonuses these days. Rookies who are considered the second coming of Orr, sign healthier ones. You can place Potvin's contract numbers in the second category. Drafted No. 1 by the Islanders, the young man agreed to a three-year contract for a reported $400,000.

General manager Bill Torrey welcomed Potvin to the Islanders, saying, "Denis has the tremendous strength to make the key play all by himself. His past performance is indicative of his offensive talents, but what makes him most valuable to our team is his ability to move the puck out of our defensive zone and up to the forwards."

Like any rookie moving up from junior hockey to the fast company of the NHL, Potvin experienced his ups and downs. He was obviously a talented young player but he sometimes exhibited rookie mistakes—on and off the ice. There was, for example, the episode of the missed bus.

The Islanders were scheduled to play a Sunday night game in Philadelphia and the club arranged for a morning bus ride down the Jersey Turnpike to their date with the Flyers. At 10:05 AM, Denis tooled his Mercedes Benz into the Nassau Coliseum parking lot. Unfortunately, the Islander bus had been scheduled to leave at 10 and, unlike the rookie defenseman, it had arrived on time.

"My mistake," said Potvin afterwards. "I overslept." Missing the bus was bad enough, but then Potvin compounded his error by returning home. He had 10 hours to cover the 90 miles between New York and Philadelphia but he panicked and missed the game instead. The faux pas cost Denis a healthy fine but also taught him an important lesson.

"The incident left a mark on Denis," said Islander Coach Al Arbour. "He won't admit it, but he was a little uptight for the next few games. He was concerned about the newspaper stories and about what the fans were thinking. He didn't want people to think he was irresponsible.

"To me, that was a good sign. He could have taken the other route, another outlook, and said the hell with the fine and the fans. That wouldn't be Denis Potvin. He does care—about the way he plays hockey and about what people think. He hasn't missed a team bus since."

Six weeks after the missed bus, low point of his rookie season, Potvin hit the other end of that emotional seesaw. He was chosen to play for the East Division All Stars against the West, the only rookie in the mid-season game. What's more, he scored a goal on a wicked 60-foot shot that buzzed by goalie Tony Esposito.

"I didn't see it go in," said Potvin afterwards, trying to reconstruct his memorable goal. "But I heard the fans roar and I knew it must be a goal. What a feeling!"

In Ottawa, Potvin's parents and his fiancee, Debbie Taylor, were watching the game on television. The house all but erupted when Denis scored. "We all started yelling," said Debbie, "yelling and running around. Even the dog started barking in the excitement."

That All Star goal and his final game four-point night had to be the best memories Potvin had of his first season with the Islanders. But they were by no means the only ones. Off the ice, Denis scooped up the fringe benefits New York has to offer.

"This is one great place," he said. "After practice, I like to drive into the city and just walk around. The museums, the theaters, what a great place. I would walk across Madison Avenue, Fifth Avenue, Radio City. I'd look at those buildings and just enjoy the whole scene."

The canyons of Manhattan had obviously captured the kid from Ottawa, every bit as completely as the kid had captured the NHL. "He is smooth," admired one rival coach. "He makes mistakes, sure, but he also overcomes them."

Potvin's Coach Al Arbour agrees with that assessment. "Denis made many mistakes and some have been costly," said the New York bench boss. "But I've used him almost 40 minutes a game and you have to expect a rookie defenseman to make plenty of errors. But he knows the mistakes when he makes them and he works so very hard in practice, trying to overcome those junior hockey habits."

Potvin recognized the problem early in his first NHL season.

"In junior hockey I was able to control play and I carried the puck when I felt like it," he said. "I did pick up some bad habits which the players in the NHL pounce on. I've learned quickly that I'm no longer the big man on the pond. I have to pick my spots to carry the puck because, many times, passing it ahead is the better move. I can't go lunging ahead to throw checks and leave a big, unguarded area in our zone. It's not that easy to adjust because I have to learn the tricks of more than the big stars. Every player here is good. There are just no easy spots."

Nobody told Denis it would be easy, least of all his brother, Jean, who was acquired by the Islanders a few months before they drafted the youngest Potvin. Jean often teamed with his brother on the New York blue line and he was asked what he thought of his rookie partner.

"I feel Denny is playing extremely well," said Jean, midway through the season. "I'd like to see him hit more, use that hip check whenever he gets a chance. Like when a player is in the corner and makes a play and tries to get out. That's when I'd like to see Denny nail the guy and keep him from moving to the net. But that will come with time. He's still feeling his way around the league, learning the different moves of the players. Once he learns that, he'll nail those guys in the corners."

Once he learns that, Denis will be back on that Orr treadmill again, challenging the Boston great as the NHL's very best defenseman.

FEATURED STARS STATISTICS

CHEEVERS, GERALD MICHAEL (GERRY)
Born, St. Catharines, Ont., December 7, 1940.
Goaltender, Shoots left 5'11", 185 lbs.
Last amateur club: St. Michael's College (Jrs.).

Regular Schedule

Season	Club	Lea	GPI	MINS	GA	SO	GAPG
1961-62	Toronto	NHL	2	120	7	0	3.50
1961-62	Sault Ste. Marie	CPHL	29		103	1	3.55
1961-62	Pitt.-Rochester	AHL	24		84	1	3.50
1962-63	Rochester	AHL	19		75	1	3.95
1962-63	Sudbury	EPHL	51		212	4	4.15
1963-64	Rochester	AHL	66		187	3	2.84
1964-65	Rochester	AHL	72		195	5	2.68
1965-66	Boston	NHL	7	340	34	0	6.00
1965-66	Oklahoma City	CPHL	30		73	3	2.49
1966-67	Boston	NHL	22	1298	72	1	3.33
1966-67	Oklahoma City	CPHL	26		71	1	2.80
1967-68	Boston	NHL	47	2646	125	3	2.83
1968-69	Boston	NHL	52	3112	145	3	2.80
1969-70	Boston	NHL	41	2384	108	4	2.72
1970-71	Boston	NHL	40	2400	109	3	2.72
1971-72	Boston	NHL	41	2420	101	2	2.50
		NHL Totals	**252**	**14720**	**701**	**16**	**2.86**
1972-73	Cleveland	WHA	52	3144	149	5	2.83
1973-74	Cleveland	WHA	59	3562	180	4	3.03
		WHA Totals	**111**	**6706**	**329**	**9**	**2.93**

CLARKE, ROBERT EARLE (BOBBY)
Born, Flin Flon, Man., August 13, 1949.
Center. Shoots left. 5'10", 180 lbs.
Last amateur club: Flin Flon Bombers (Jrs.).

Regular Schedule

Season	Club	Lea	GP	G	A	TP	PIM
1969-70	Philadelphia	NHL	76	15	31	46	68
1970-71	Philadelphia	NHL	77	27	36	63	78
1971-72	Philadelphia	NHL	78	35	46	81	87
1972-73	Philadelphia	NHL	78	37	67	104	80
1973-74	Philadelphia	NHL	77	35	52	87	113
		NHL Totals	**386**	**149**	**232**	**381**	**426**

COURNOYER, YVAN SERGE

Born, Drummondville, Que., November 22, 1943.
Right wing. Shoots left. 5'7", 165 lbs.
Last amateur club: Montreal Canadiens (Jrs.)

Regular Schedule

Season	Club	Lea	GP	G	A	TP	PIM
1963-64	Mtl. Canadiens	NHL	5	4	0	4	0
1964-65	Quebec	AHL	7	2	1	3	0
1964-65	Mtl. Canadiens	NHL	55	7	10	17	10
1965-66	Mtl. Canadiens	NHL	65	18	11	29	8
1966-67	Mtl. Canadiens	NHL	69	25	15	40	14
1967-68	Mtl. Canadiens	NHL	64	28	32	60	23
1968-69	Mtl. Canadiens	NHL	76	43	44	87	31
1969-70	Mtl. Canadiens	NHL	72	27	36	63	23
1970-71	Mtl. Canadiens	NHL	65	37	36	73	21
1971-72	Mtl. Canadiens	NHL	73	47	36	83	15
1972-73	Mtl. Canadiens	NHL	67	40	39	79	18
1973-74	Mtl. Canadiens	NHL	67	40	33	73	18
		NHL Totals	**668**	**316**	**292**	**608**	**181**

ESPOSITO, PHILIP ANTHONY (PHIL)

Born, Sault Ste. Marie, Ont., February 20, 1942.
Center. Shoots left. 6'1", 210 lbs.
Last amateur club: St. Catharines Teepes (Jrs.)

Regular Schedule

Season	Club	Lea	GP	G	A	TP	PIM
1961-62	Sault Ste. Marie	EPHL	6	0	3	3	2
1962-63	St. Louis	EPHL	71	36	54	90	51
1963-64	St. Louis	CPHL	43	26	54	80	65
1963-64	Chicago	NHL	27	3	2	5	2
1964-65	Chicago	NHL	70	23	32	55	44
1965-66	Chicago	NHL	69	27	26	53	49
1966-67	Chicago	NHL	69	21	40	61	40
1967-68	Boston	NHL	74	35	49	84	21
1968-69	Boston	NHL	74	49	77	126	79
1969-70	Boston	NHL	76	43	56	99	50
1970-71	Boston	NHL	78	76	76	152	71
1971-72	Boston	NHL	76	66	67	133	76
1972-73	Boston	NHL	78	55	75	130	87
1973-74	Boston	NHL	78	68	77	145	58
		NHL Totals	**769**	**466**	**577**	**1043**	**567**

ESPOSITO, ANTHONY JAMES (TONY)
Born, Sault Ste. Marie, Ont., April 23, 1943.
Goaltender, Shoots right. 5'11", 185 lbs.
Last amateur club: Michigan Tech.

Regular Schedule

Season	Club	Lea	GPI	MINS	GA	SO	GAPG
1967-68	Vancouver	WHL	63	3734	199	4	3.20
1968-69	Mtl. Canadiens	NHL	13	746	34	2	2.73
1968-69	Houston	CHL	19	1139	46	1	2.42
1969-70	Chicago	NHL	63	3763	136	15	2.17
1970-71	Chicago	NHL	57	3325	126	6	2.27
1971-72	Chicago	NHL	48	2780	82	9	1.76
1972-73	Chicago	NHL	56	3340	140	4	2.51
1973-74	Chicago	NHL	70	4143	141	10	2.04
		NHL Totals	**307**	**18097**	**659**	**46**	**2.18**

GILBERT, RODRIGUE GABRIEL (ROD)
Born, Montreal, Que., July 1, 1941
Right wing. Shoots right. 5'9", 175 lbs.
Last amateur club: Guelph Royals (Jrs.)

Regular Schedule

Season	Club	Lea	GP	G	A	TP	PIM
1959-60	Three Rivers	EPHL	3	4	6	10	0
1960-61	NY Rangers	NHL	1	0	1	1	2
1961-62	Kitch.-Waterloo	EPHL	21	12	11	23	22
1961-62	NY Rangers	NHL	1	0	0	0	0
1962-63	NY Rangers	NHL	70	11	20	31	20
1963-64	NY Rangers	NHL	70	24	40	64	62
1964-65	NY Rangers	NHL	70	25	36	61	52
1965-66	NY Rangers	NHL	34	10	15	25	20
1966-67	NY Rangers	NHL	64	28	18	46	12
1967-68	NY Rangers	NHL	73	29	48	77	12
1968-69	NY Rangers	NHL	66	28	49	77	22
1969-70	NY Rangers	NHL	72	16	37	53	22
1970-71	NY Rangers	NHL	78	30	31	61	65
1971-72	NY Rangers	NHL	73	43	54	97	64
1972-73	NY Rangers	NHL	76	25	59	84	25
1973-74	NY Rangers	NHL	75	36	41	77	20
		NHL Totals	**823**	**305**	**449**	**754**	**398**

HULL, ROBERT MARVIN (BOBBY)
Born, Point Anne, Ont., January 3, 1939.
Left wing. Shoots left. 5'10", 193 lbs.
Last amateur club: St. Catharines Black Hawks (Jrs.)

Regular Schedule

Season	Club	Lea	GP	G	A	TP	PIM
1957-58	Chicago	NHL	70	13	34	47	62
1958-59	Chicago	NHL	70	18	32	50	50

1959-60	Chicago	NHL	70	39	42	81	68
1960-61	Chicago	NHL	67	31	25	56	43
1961-62	Chicago	NHL	70	50	34	84	35
1962-63	Chicago	NHL	65	31	31	62	27
1963-64	Chicago	NHL	70	43	44	87	50
1964-65	Chicago	NHL	61	39	32	71	32
1965-66	Chicago	NHL	65	54	43	97	70
1966-67	Chicago	NHL	66	52	28	80	52
1967-68	Chicago	NHL	71	44	31	75	39
1968-69	Chicago	NHL	74	58	49	107	48
1969-70	Chicago	NHL	61	38	29	67	8
1970-71	Chicago	NHL	78	44	52	96	32
1971-72	Chicago	NHL	78	50	43	93	24
		NHL Totals	**1036**	**604**	**549**	**1153**	**640**
1972	Winnipeg	WHA	63	51	52	103	37
1973-74	Winnipeg	WHA	75	53	42	95	38
		WHA Totals	**138**	**104**	**94**	**198**	**75**

MARTIN, RICHARD LIONEL

Born, Verdun, Que., July 26, 1951.
Left wing. Shoots left. 5'11", 170 lbs.
Last amateur club: Montreal Canadiens (Jrs.)

Regular Schedule

Season	**Club**	**Lea**	**GP**	**G**	**A**	**TP**	**PIM**
1971-72	Buffalo	NHL	73	44	30	74	36
1972-73	Buffalo	NHL	75	37	36	73	79
1973-74	Buffalo	NHL	78	52	34	86	38
		NHL Totals	**226**	**133**	**100**	**233**	**153**

ORR, ROBERT GORDON (BOBBY)

Born, Parry Sound, Ont., March 20, 1948.
Defense. Shoots left. 5'11", 185 lbs.
Last amateur club: Oshawa Generals (Jrs.).

Regular Schedule

Season	**Club**	**Lea**	**GP**	**G**	**A**	**TP**	**PIM**
1966-67 a	Boston	NHL	61	13	28	41	102
1967-68 b	Boston	NHL	46	11	20	31	63
1968-69 b	Boston	NHL	67	21	43	64	133
1969-70	Boston	NHL	76	33	87	120	125
1970-71	Boston	NHL	78	37	102	139	91
1971-72	Boston	NHL	76	37	80	117	106
1972-73	Boston	NHL	63	29	72	101	99
1973-74	Boston	NHL	74	32	90	122	82
		NHL Totals	**541**	**213**	**522**	**735**	**801**

PARENT, BERNARD MARCEL (BERNIE)
Born, Montreal, Que., April 3, 1945.
Goaltender. Shoots left. 5'11", 180 lbs.
Last amateur club: Niagara Falls Flyers (Jrs.).

Regular Schedule

Season	Club	Lea	GPI	MINS	GA	SO	GAPG
1965-66	Oklahoma City	CPHL	3		11	0	3.67
1965-66	Boston	NHL	39	2083	128	1	3.69
1966-67	Boston	NHL	18	1022	62	0	3.64
1966-67	Oklahoma City	CPHL	14		37	4	2.70
1967-68	Philadelphia	NHL	38	2248	93	4	2.49
1968-69	Philadelphia	NHL	58	3365	151	1	2.69
1969-70	Philadelphia	NHL	62	3680	171	3	2.79
1970-71	Philadelphia	NHL	30	1586	73	2	2.76
	Toronto	NHL	18	1040	46	1	2.65
1971-72	Toronto	NHL	47	2715	116	3	2.56
1973-74	Philadelphia	NHL	73	4314	136	12	1.89
		NHL Totals	**383**	**22053**	**976**	**27**	**2.63**
1972-73	Philadelphia	WHA	63	3653	220	2	3.61
		WHA Totals	**63**	**3653**	**220**	**2**	**3.61**

PARK, DOUGLAS BRADFORD (BRAD)
Born, Toronto, Ont., July 6, 1948.
Defense Shoots left. 6', 190 lbs.
Last amateur club: Toronto Marlboros (Jrs.)

Regular Schedule

Season	Club	Lea	GP	G	A	TP	PIM
1968-69	Buffalo	AHL	17	2	12	14	49
1968-69	NY Rangers	NHL	54	3	23	26	70
1969-70	NY Rangers	NHL	60	11	26	37	98
1970-71	NY Rangers	NHL	68	7	37	44	114
1971-72	NY Rangers	NHL	75	24	49	73	130
1972-73	NY Rangers	NHL	52	10	43	53	51
1973-74	NY Rangers	NHL	78	25	57	82	148
		NHL Totals	**387**	**80**	**235**	**315**	**611**

POTVIN, DENIS
Born, Hull, Que., October 29, 1953
Defense. Shoots left. 6', 204 lbs.
Last amateur club: Ottawa 67s (Jrs.)

Regular Schedule

Season	Club	Lea	GP	G	A	TP	PIM
1973-74	NY Islanders	NHL	77	17	37	54	175
		NHL Totals	**77**	**17**	**37**	**54**	**175**

REVIEWS

NHL REVIEW

It was the kind of goal that comes only from hard work. It was the kind of goal the Flyers had been scoring all year.

Rick MacLeish won the faceoff, drawing the puck to Moose Dupont at the left point. While Dupont sent the puck towards the net, MacLeish skated to the goaltender's left. The puck and MacLeish's stick arrived at the same time and before Gilles Gilbert or defenseman Dallas Smith could react, the Philadelphia Flyers had a 1-0 lead over the Boston Bruins in the Stanley Cup's deciding game

That was to be the goal that sent the Cup to the Flyers, called bullies and hooligans by some and "the greatest team I've ever seen," by their coach, Fred Shero.

"Sure, you'd get more on the open market for Bobby Orr than Orest Kindrachuk or Terry Crisp, you'd get more for Phil Esposito than Bill Clement, but it takes 17 men to make a hockey team," Shero said when the Cup became Philadelphia property.

It became Philadelphia property thanks to Shero and a dedicated bunch of players who didn't stop skating, scrapping, scrambling or scoring until they had enough goals to scratch their names on Lord Stanley's silverware.

Said goaltender Bernie Parent, the playoffs' Most Valuable Player, "We are not the most talented team ever to win this thing by a long shot. It is the result of hard work. You don't realize how much damn hard work we put in for this thing and that is what makes it such a great experience. Even if you had a hundred million dollars, you cannot buy the feeling that we have right now."

The Flyers' Cup came from many ingredients. It was Coach Shero driving his club in practices; it was Bobby Clarke setting up the plays, Dave Schultz provoking the trouble, Parent adamantly stingy about giving up goals, and

20

Bernie Parent makes the kick save to stop Boston again. Parent's goaltending led Philadelphia to the Stanley Cup against the Bruins.

the ever-present defense hitting everything that moved.

That was the winning formula. Only one team could have it and last year, the Flyers did.

For the rest of the league, there was frustration —especially for the so-called established teams, which showed signs of agreeing (hesitantly, of course), that the young West Division had arrived.

For the New York Rangers, there was another maddening playoff loss. In Montreal, inconsistency and injuries killed Cup chances; Boston, except for the tireless Bobby Orr, seemed to lack motivation when it was so badly needed.

Chicago's Black Hawks again were playoff bridesmaids, losing first place in the West to the Flyers before losing the playoff semifinals to Boston. Toronto just didn't have the talent for a concerted run at the Cup, but surprising clubs in Los Angeles and Atlanta gave pause for thought about the future.

Then, of course, there were the teams whose futures were many years off. California continued to struggle like a ship without a captain; Minnesota won 23 of 78 games—only four more than the second-year Islanders; Buffalo suffered throughout the season: first severe injuries to Gilbert Perreault and young Jim Schoenfeld, then the crushing death in an auto crash of veteran Tim Horton.

Detroit, having tried everything else, made 20-year veteran Alex Delvecchio its bench coach; Vancouver went through coaches, general managers, players, you name it . . . nothing worked at all. The same was true in St. Louis and Pittsburgh, where the Blues and Penguins dug holes so deep that it was just too late to recover by the time each had a new coach.

To hear the coaches tell it, the season was a gloomy one.

ITEM: Jean-Guy Talbot, on resigning his position with the Blues, said, "I wasn't eating, I wasn't sleeping and I would get pains in my chest in the middle of the night. The strain was beginning to affect me and my family, and I'm only 41 years old."

Opponents scored 100 less goals against Islanders last year, thanks largely to efforts of Rookie of the Year Denis Potvin.

10
21

Ranger Pete Stemkowski (21) follows Chicago's Dennis Hull (10) while goalie Tony Esposito keeps an eye on things.

ITEM: Jack Gordon, on resigning as coach of the Minnesota North Stars: "The pressure got on my nerves more and more. The response was not there. I was not getting the message to the players."

ITEM: Larry Popein, after being relieved of his coaching duties with the Rangers by general manager Emile Francis—the third time Francis has had to take over for a coach in the middle of a season: "I knew I was going into the bees' nest with the queen still there. I had my doubts the day I was offered the job."

What a change from the past! The day of absolute rule by National Hockey League coaches seems to have come to a startling end. More and more, players were rebelling against them.

Maybe that's why last season took the shape it did. It seemed no coach was safe in his job, and that insecurity had its effect on the players.

In Pittsburgh, incoming coach Marc Boileau noticed "When I took over these guys had stopped believing in themselves. They were expecting to lose and that was one of the reasons why they were losing."

In Boston, deposed Coach Bep Guidolin cited scoring superstar Phil Esposito as one of the Bruin troublemakers. During a game in St. Louis, he gave an order to Esposito on the bench and Esposito simply turned around and told him to get lost. Later, in the dressing room, the two exchanged angry words.

In other cities, coach and club reached a happy medium. And it was in those cities where seemingly unattainable successes took place.

Atlanta is a prime example. A young Flames team worked with—instead of against—Coach Bernie Geoffrion, and made the playoffs in only its second year of existence. Despite the fact they lost four straight to the Cup-bound Flyers in the playoffs, Geoffrion was given an extension on his contract and the scrappy Flames made it known that improvement was imminent.

Philadelphia's Bobby Clarke (left) and Keith Magnuson of Chicago battle for the puck.

In Los Angeles, Bob Pulford rallied his Kings to a sturdy performance in the playoffs, although credit also is due Jake Milford, who left the New York Rangers' staff to become Kings general manager and engineered a couple of deals which made that performance possible.

One of the deals was with his former club. Milford parted with hard-hitting defenseman Gilles Marotte and the marginally talented Real Lemieux, and received youngsters with futures: Mike Murphy, Tommy Williams and Sheldon Kannegiesser. Another deal with the Rangers brought potential star Gene Carr from the gray East Coast to the sunny West.

The trades worked fine for the Kings, whom all thought were building for the future. But in New York, there was considerable criticism. From the corner bar to the mezzanine at Madison Square Garden, Rangers fans moaned again.

Frustrated by the team's most recent playoff failures, the Ranger fan jumped on any negative incident to clamor for a shake-up. Francis had made trades like the one with the Kings before: sending a youngster with a promising future to another club and receiving in return a player of less than exceptional ability.

Another factor that piqued the Ranger fan was the outrageous salaries Francis had offered in 1972-73 to keep his veterans from jumping to the World Hockey Association. They saw the team as an aging bunch of fat-cats who didn't bother to try as hard as the Flyers or Flames. And then, of course, there was the grating, seven-game loss to the Flyers in the playoff semifinal—a loss to a team that had been in the league a mere seven years.

Francis, finally, would give in to the clamor, trading high-priced left wing Vic Hadfield to the Penguins for Nick Beverley, a little known defenseman who would be much easier on the Rangers' budget.

Then came the big move: the acquisition of Derek Sanderson from the Bruins. Sanderson, the brash center who invited controversy and anything else into the world of pro hockey, was as different from Francis as hockey is from baseball. Francis doesn't permit his players to wear mustaches; Sanderson has one. Francis doesn't allow smoking in the dressing room; Sanderson always smokes in the dressing room. Francis likes his players' hair short; Sanderson keeps his coiffed in the latest styles.

New York's Steve Vickers (8) and Rod Gilbert (7) have Buffalo defenseman Larry Carriere surrounded.

Yet for all their differences—and those listed above were only a few—each had expressed an admiration for the other.

It seemed to be the eye in the storm that was Sanderson's career. The Bruins suspended him for the remainder of last season on March 10 after he twice fought with teammate Terry O'Reilly in the dressing room in Oakland, then missed the team plane back to Boston the next day. Other times, the capricious center was criticized for lack of hustle, praised for outstanding work on faceoffs, admonished for his lack of discipline and admired by a number of fans.

The Bruins, however, got along without Sanderson. They cruised into first place in the East Division with 113 points—14 more than second-place Montreal—on the

Toronto's Ron Ellis shoots . . . and scores against Montreal.

strength of another patented Esposito season: 68 goals, 77 assists, 145 points. Bobby Orr's 32 goals and 90 assists didn't hurt, nor did 105 points by Ken Hodge or the Bruins' 33-4-2 record at home during the regular season.

The Canadiens couldn't claim exceptional statistics like those. Frank Mahovlich led their scorers with only 80 points, and it was seven points back to Yvan Cournoyer and Frank's

brother Pete, who tied for second with 73. The old Montreal magic at home dissipated somewhat, too, as the Canadiens went 24-12-3.

The goaltending magic of Ken Dryden was gone . . . at least temporarily, and it showed up in the disappointing second-place finish. Dryden decided to sit out the season when Habs' general manager Sam Pollock wouldn't meet his salary demands. Because you don't find a goaltender off the street with a career 2.22 goals-against average, Montreal was hard-pressed to replace the 6-foot-4 netminder.

They rotated Michel Plasse, Michel Larocque and Wayne Thomas, but despite a fine series by Larocque in the six-game loss to New York in the playoff semifinals, none of the goalies pleased the front office.

The Maple Leafs tried to rotate three goalies, too, and made the playoffs after a year's absence with the help of two rookies from Sweden. Defenseman Borje Salming and winger Inge Hammarstrom were impressive in their first year of hockey in North America. Center Darryl Sittler did what has been of expected of him and finished with 84 points. Veterans anchored the squad on the way to fourth place: Norm Ullman contributed 69 points while Paul Henderson, Ron Ellis and Dave Keon followed. Eddie Johnston shared the goaltending with Doug Favell and Dunc Wilson, leading the Leafs to the second-lowest goals-against total in the East Division—230. Boston surrendered nine fewer goals to lead the East.

For Buffalo, the season was marred by numerous setbacks. The Sabres reeled when Perreault broke his leg; the brilliant center still managed to play in 55 games and score 51 points. Schoenfeld's back problem hurt the club considerably, goaltender Roger Crozier was hospitalized with recurring stomach troubles, and then came the death of Horton—one of the most respected men in hockey. It was too much for the Sabres to overcome.

Richard Martin provided a bright spot with 86 points, including 52 goals. Defenseman Larry Carriere showed strength on defense and the acquisition of Jerry Korab, an aggressive 6-foot-3, 215 pounder, gave Sabre fans plenty to look forward to.

The Red Wings had a tough time getting it all together, but the play of Mickey Redmond (51 goals) and Marcel Dionne gave some hope for the future. Detroit just couldn't find a solution to its defensive and goaltending problems until Jim

Chicago's Stan Mikita (21) ranks as one of hockey's finest centers.

Rutherford started guarding the goal regularly. But Rutherford couldn't keep the Wings from giving 319 goals—better only than the hapless Seals, who gave up 342. Reports of dissension provided the off-the-ice problems for Detroit, resulting in the firing of coach Ted Garvin early in the season

Cliff Koroll of the Black Hawks lifts puck past fallen Bobby Orr (4) and into Boston's net.

and the resignation of controversial general manager Ned Harkness. The Wings started off with a 2-9-1 record before dismissing the outspoken Garvin.

Confusion reigned in Vancouver, which beat out the New York Islanders for seventh place in the East by only three points. There was a revolving door to the front office, with the occupants leaving often. Phil Maloney was the general manager who came into office at just about the time his club's most popular player, Bobby Schmautz, was traded to the Boston Bruins for Chris Oddleifson and Fred O'Donnell. Instead of joining the Canucks, O'Donnell jumped to the WHA. Things got so bad that at one point, goaltender Gary Smith just walked out.

The team was headed for Chicago and the third stop of a three-stop road trip. Smith, reportedly fed up with front office developments, refused to go to Chicago and was missing from the team for a while.

The Islanders at times played like most of their team was missing. Indeed, it was missing—missing passes, missing line changes, even missing buses. One day, rookie sensation Denis Potvin missed the team bus to Philadelphia. He overslept; and upon awakening, realized what happened. Too upset to drive to Philadelphia himself, Potvin stayed home and watched the game on television.

Other times, Potvin showed the promise that will someday help make the Islanders something other than the doormats of the East Division. He led the team in scoring with 17 goals and 37 assists, and along with tough youngsters such as Bobby Nystrom, Gary Howatt, Billy Harris and Ralph Stewart will probably bring respectability to suburban New York hockey fans.

Chicago was tied up in knots. As if 23 ties during the regular season weren't enough, goaltender Tony Esposito ended up tied with Philadelphia's Parent for the Vezina Trophy. Detroit's Marcel Dionne scored on Esposito with only 66 seconds remaining in the season. It was the 164th goal the Black Hawks allowed—same as the Flyers. So both

The anguish of a goaltender. Tony Esposito has just let one get past him.

names went on the treasured trophy.

The Hawks were easily the best road team last season, finishing with 21 victories and 10 ties in their 39 games away from home. Stan Mikita collected 30 goals and 50 assists to lead Hawks scorers. Pit Martin had three fewer assists for 77 points, and Jim Pappin was third with 73.

All the scoring and goaltending did not amount to much in Chicago, where the Black Hawk Esposito lost a semifinal playoff decision to the Boston Esposito and the Bruins eliminated Chicago in six games.

New York beat Montreal in their first-round battle, thanks to an excellent performance by goaltender Ed Giacomin, who hit almost as many Canadiens as the Rangers defense did. As mentioned earlier, Larocque was nearly as good in the Montreal cage, but injuries to defenseman Jacques Laperierre and other Canadiens were impossible to overcome.

But the Rangers tasted defeat—again—when they met the Flyers, who had breezed past the Flames in four games. That set up the big final series with the Bruins.

And in the sixth game, with the Spectrum in a frenzy, there happened to be a penalty to Boston's Terry O'Reilly. With O'Reilly in the penalty box and a faceoff in the Boston end, Rick MacLeish won the draw and sent the puck to Moose Dupont at the left point.

There's no point going on. You know the Flyers won it all.

1973-74 NHL STANDINGS AND STATISTICS

EAST DIVISION

	GP	W	L	T	GF	GA	Pts
Boston	78	52	17	9	349	221	113
Montreal	78	45	24	9	293	240	99
NY Rangers	78	40	24	14	300	251	94
Toronto	78	35	27	16	274	230	86
Buffalo	78	32	34	12	242	250	76
Detroit	78	29	39	10	255	319	68
Vancouver	78	24	43	11	224	296	59
NY Islanders	78	19	41	18	182	247	56

WEST DIVISION

	GP	W	L	T	GF	GA	Pts
Philadelphia	78	50	16	12	273	164	112
Chicago	78	41	14	23	272	164	105
Los Angeles	78	33	33	12	233	231	78
Atlanta	78	30	34	14	214	238	74
Pittsburgh	78	28	41	9	242	273	65
St. Louis	78	26	40	12	206	248	64
Minnesota	78	23	38	17	235	275	63
California	78	13	55	10	195	342	36

INDIVIDUAL SCORING LEADERS

Player	Team	GP	G	A	Pts	Pim
Phil Esposito	Bost.	78	68	77	145	58
Bobby Orr	Bost.	74	32	90	122	82
Ken Hodge	Bost.	76	50	55	105	43
Wayne Cashman	Bost.	78	30	59	89	111
Bobby Clarke	Phila.	77	35	52	87	113
Richard Martin	Buff.	78	52	34	86	38
Syl Apps	Pitts.	75	24	61	85	37
Darryl Sittler	Tor.	78	38	46	84	55
Lowell MacDonald	Pitts.	78	43	39	82	14
Brad Park	Rangers	78	25	57	82	148
Dennis Hextall	Minn.	78	20	62	82	138
Frank Mahovlich	Mont.	71	31	49	80	47
Stan Mikita	Chi.	76	30	50	80	46
Marcel Dionne	Det.	74	24	54	78	10
Mickey Redmond	Det.	76	51	26	77	14
Rod Gilbert	Rangers	75	36	41	77	20
Rick Macleish	Phila.	78	32	45	77	42
Pit Martin	Chi.	78	30	47	77	43
John Bucyk	Bost.	76	31	44	75	8
Andre Boudrias	Van.	78	16	59	75	18
Bill Goldsworthy	Minn.	74	48	26	74	73
Yvan Cournoyer	Mont.	67	40	33	73	18
Pete Mahovlich	Mont.	78	36	37	73	122
Jim Pappin	Chi.	78	32	41	73	76
Jean Pronovost	Pitts.	77	40	32	72	22

ATLANTA

	GP	G	A	Pts	Pim
Tom Lysiak	77	19	45	64	54
Al McDonough	72	24	31	55	27
Bob Leiter	78	26	26	52	10
Larry Romanchych	73	22	29	51	33
Jacques Richard	78	27	16	43	45
Curt Bennett	71	17	24	41	34
Keith McCreary	76	18	19	37	62
Randy Manery	78	8	29	37	75
Rey Comeau	78	11	23	34	16
John Stewart	74	18	15	33	41
Pat Quinn	77	5	27	32	94
Leon Rochefort	56	10	12	22	13
Bryan Hextall	77	4	11	15	94
Noel Price	62	0	13	13	38
Eric Vail	23	2	9	11	30
Jean Lemieux	32	3	5	8	6
Arnie Brown	48	2	6	8	29
Butch Deadmarsh	42	6	1	7	89
Lew Morrison	52	1	4	5	0
Doug Mohns	28	0	3	3	10
Bob Murray	62	0	3	3	34
Ed Kea	3	0	2	2	0
Don Martineau	4	0	0	0	2
Dwight Bialowas	11	0	0	0	2
Phil Myre	36	0	0	0	4
Dan Bouchard	46	0	0	0	10

BOSTON

	GP	G	A	Pts	Pim
Phil Esposito	78	68	77	145	58
Bobby Orr	74	32	90	122	82
Ken Hodge	76	50	55	105	43
Wayne Cashman	78	30	59	89	111
John Bucyk	76	31	44	75	8
Bobby Schmautz	76	33	32	65	89
Carol Vadnais	78	16	43	59	121
Don Marcotte	78	24	26	50	18
Gregg Sheppard	76	16	31	47	21
Terry O'Reilly	76	11	24	35	94
Andre Savard	72	16	14	30	39
Dallas Smith	77	6	21	27	64
Dave Forbes	63	10	16	26	41
Derek Sanderson	29	8	12	20	48
Al Sims	76	3	9	12	22
Darryl Edestrand	55	3	8	11	20
Rich Leduc	28	3	3	6	12
Gary Doak	69	0	4	4	44
Ken Broderick	5	0	1	1	0
Gilles Gilbert	54	0	1	1	9
Ross Brooks	2	0	0	0	2
Bob Gryp	1	0	0	0	0
Doug Gibson	2	0	0	0	0
Dave Hynes	3	0	0	0	0
Al Simmons	3	0	0	0	0

BUFFALO

	GP	G	A	Pts	Pim
Richard Martin	78	52	34	86	38
Rene Robert	76	21	44	65	71
Don Luce	75	26	31	57	44
Jim Lorentz	78	23	31	54	28
Gil Perreault	55	18	33	51	10
Gerry Meehan	72	20	26	46	17
Craig Ramsay	78	20	26	46	0
Larry Carriere	78	6	24	30	103
Jerry Korab	76	10	19	29	137
Rick Dudley	67	13	13	26	71
Brian Spencer	67	8	18	26	69
Mike Robitaille	71	2	18	20	60
Norm Gratton	57	6	11	17	16
Steve Atkinson	70	6	10	16	22
Paul Terbenche	67	2	12	14	8
Peter McNab	22	3	6	9	2
Jim Schoenfeld	28	1	8	9	56
Larry Mickey	13	3	4	7	8
Tim Horton	55	0	6	6	53
Ron Busniuk	5	0	3	3	4
Real Lemieux	38	1	1	2	4
Bill Hajt	6	0	2	2	0
Randy Wyrozub	5	0	1	1	0
Dave Dryden	53	0	1	1	4
Rocky Farr	11	0	0	0	2
Gary Bromley	12	0	0	0	2
Roger Crozier	12	0	0	0	2
Joe Noris	18	0	0	0	2

CALIFORNIA

	GP	G	A	Pts	Pim
Joey Johnston	78	27	40	67	67
Ivan Boldirev	78	25	31	56	22
Walt McKechnie	63	23	29	52	14
Reg Leach	78	22	24	46	34
Gary Croteau	76	14	21	35	16
Stan Gilbertson	76	18	12	30	39
Craig Patrick	59	10	20	30	17
Hilliard Graves	64	11	18	29	48
Morris Mott	77	9	17	26	33
Ted McAneeley	72	4	20	24	62
Marshall Johnston	50	2	16	18	24
Stan Weir	58	9	7	16	10
Pete Laframboise	65	7	7	14	14
Ray McKay	72	2	12	14	49
Ron Huston	23	3	10	13	0
Terry Murray	58	0	12	12	48
Brent Meeke	18	1	9	10	4
Rick Kessell	51	2	6	8	4
Bob Stewart	47	2	5	7	69
Paul Shakes	21	0	4	4	12
Barry Cummins	36	1	2	3	39
Del Hall	2	2	0	2	2
Lyle Bradley	4	1	0	1	2
Marv Edwards	14	0	1	1	4
Gilles Meloche	47	0	1	1	2
Bruce Greig	1	0	0	0	4

Gary Holt	1	0	0	0	0
Hartland Monahan	1	0	0	0	0
Larry Patey	1	0	0	0	0
Dave Hrechkosy	2	0	0	0	0
Wayne King	2	0	0	0	0
Ron Serafini	2	0	0	0	2

CHICAGO

	GP	G	A	Pts	Pim
Stan Mikita	76	30	50	80	46
Pit Martin	78	30	47	77	43
Jim Pappin	78	32	41	73	76
Dennis Hull	74	29	39	68	15
Dick Redmond	76	17	42	59	69
Cliff Koroll	78	21	25	46	32
Germain Gagnon	76	11	28	39	12
Bill White	69	5	31	36	52
Phil Russell	75	10	25	35	184
Dale Tallon	65	15	19	34	36
Chico Maki	69	9	25	34	12
Darcy Rota	74	21	12	33	58
John Marks	76	13	18	31	22
Lynn Powis	57	8	13	21	6
J.P. Bordeleau	64	11	9	20	11
Dave Kryskow	72	7	12	19	22
Doug Jarrett	67	5	11	16	45
Len Frig	66	4	10	14	35
Keith Magnuson	57	2	11	13	105
Mike Veisor	10	0	1	1	0
Tony Esposito	70	0	1	1	0
Gary Donaldson	1	0	0	0	0
Rob Palmer	1	0	0	0	0

DETROIT

	GP	G	A	Pts	Pim
Marcel Dionne	74	24	54	78	10
Mickey Redmond	76	51	26	77	14
Red Berenson	76	24	42	66	28
Guy Charron	76	25	30	55	10
Nick Libett	67	24	24	48	37
Pierre Jarry	64	17	31	48	27
Bill Hogaboam	47	18	23	41	12
Doug Roberts	64	12	26	38	35
Henry Boucha	70	19	12	31	32
Brent Hughes	70	1	21	22	92
Jack Lynch	52	3	16	19	48
Larry Johnston	65	2	12	14	139
Chris Evans	77	4	9	13	10
Bryan Watson	70	1	9	10	255
Robbie Ftorek	12	2	5	7	4
Tom Mellor	25	2	4	6	25
Nelson Debenedet	15	4	1	5	2
Alex Delvecchio	11	1	4	5	2
Jean Hamel	45	1	4	5	46
Allan McLeod	26	2	2	4	24
Dan Gruen	18	1	3	4	7
Blair Stewart	17	0	4	4	0
Jim Rutherford	51	0	4	4	4

Thommie Bergman	43	0	3	3	21
Tord Lundstrom	11	1	1	2	0
Murray Wing	1	0	1	1	0
Len Fontaine	7	0	1	1	4
Terry Richardson	9	0	1	1	0
Mike Korney	2	0	0	0	0
Rick Newell	3	0	0	0	0
Brian Lavender	4	0	0	0	11
Nelson Pyatt	5	0	0	0	0
Rick Foley	7	0	0	0	4
Bill McKenzie	13	0	0	0	2
Doug Grant	37	0	0	0	2

LOS ANGELES

	GP	G	A	Pts	Pim
Butch Goring	78	28	33	61	2
Whitey Widing	71	27	30	57	26
Bob Berry	77	23	33	56	56
Bob Nevin	78	20	30	50	12
Frank St. Marseille	78	14	36	50	40
Mike Corrigan	75	16	26	42	119
Don Kozak	76	21	14	35	54
Dan Mahoney	65	15	17	32	113
Mike Murphy	68	15	17	32	38
Tom Williams	60	12	19	31	10
Bob Murdoch	76	8	20	28	85
S. Kannegeisser	63	4	20	24	55
Gene Carr	50	7	16	23	51
Barry Long	60	3	19	22	118
Terry Harper	77	0	17	17	119
Randy Rota	58	10	6	16	16
Vic Venasky	32	6	5	11	12
Neil Komadoski	68	2	4	6	43
Phil Hoene	31	2	3	5	22
Larry Brown	45	0	4	4	14
Bill Lesuk	35	2	1	3	32
Jimmy Peters	25	2	0	2	0
Gary Edwards	18	0	0	0	12
Rogie Vachon	65	0	0	0	6

MINNESOTA

	GP	G	A	Pts	Pim
Dennis Hextall	78	20	62	82	138
Bill Goldsworthy	74	48	26	74	73
Danny Grant	78	29	35	64	16
J.P. Parise	78	18	37	55	42
Fred Stanfield	71	16	28	44	10
Jude Drouin	65	19	24	43	30
Barry Gibbs	76	9	29	38	82
Murray Oliver	78	17	20	37	4
Buster Harvey	72	16	17	33	14
Lou Nanne	76	11	21	32	46
Gary Bergman	68	3	29	32	84
Tom Reid	76	4	19	23	81
Tony Featherstone	54	9	12	21	4
Dennis O'Brien	77	5	12	17	166
Gary Gambucci	42	1	7	8	9
Fred Barrett	40	0	7	7	12

Alain Langlais	14	3	3	6	8
Johnny Rogers	10	2	4	6	0
Dean Prentice	24	2	3	5	4
Terry Holbrook	22	1	3	4	4
Rod Norrish	9	2	1	3	0
Rick Chinnick	1	0	1	1	0
Chris Ahrens	3	0	1	1	0
Bill Plager	1	0	0	0	2
Jerry Byers	10	0	0	0	0
Blake Dunlop	12	0	0	0	2
Cesare Maniago	40	0	0	0	2

MONTREAL

	GP	G	A	Pts	Pim
Frank Mahovlich	71	31	49	80	47
Yvan Cournoyer	67	40	33	73	18
Pete Mahovlich	78	36	37	73	122
Jacques Lemaire	66	29	38	67	10
Guy Lafleur	73	21	35	56	29
Henri Richard	75	19	36	55	28
Chuck Lefley	74	23	31	54	34
Guy Lapointe	71	13	40	53	63
Steve Shutt	70	15	20	35	17
Murray Wilson	72	17	14	31	26
Larry Robinson	78	6	20	26	66
Claude Larose	39	17	7	24	52
Jim Roberts	67	8	16	24	39
Serge Savard	67	4	14	18	49
Yvon Lambert	60	6	10	16	42
Pierre Bouchard	60	1	14	15	25
Jacques Laperriere	42	2	10	12	14
Bob Gainey	66	3	7	10	34
John Van Boxmeer	20	1	4	5	18
Richard Wilson	21	0	2	2	6
Michel Larocque	27	0	2	2	0
Wayne Thomas	42	0	2	2	6
Glenn Goldup	6	0	0	0	0

N.Y. ISLANDERS

	GP	G	A	Pts	Pim
Denis Potvin	77	17	37	54	175
Bill Harris	78	23	27	50	34
Ralph Stewart	67	23	20	43	6
Ed Westfall	68	19	23	42	28
Bob Nystrom	77	21	20	41	118
Craig Cameron	78	15	14	29	28
Jean Potvin	78	5	23	28	100
Lorne Henning	60	12	15	27	6
Doug Rombough	58	9	10	19	35
Gary Howatt	78	6	11	17	204
Dave Lewis	68	2	15	17	58
Andre St. Laurent	42	5	9	14	18
Ernie Hicke	55	6	7	13	26
Bill Macmillan	55	4	9	13	16
Dave Hudson	63	2	10	12	7
Gerry Hart	70	1	10	11	61
Bert Marshall	69	1	7	8	84
Tom Miller	19	2	1	3	4

Bob Cook	22	2	1	3	4
Skeeter Teal	1	0	0	0	0
Brian Marchinko	6	0	0	0	0
Bryan Lefley	7	0	0	0	0
Neil Nicholson	8	0	0	0	0
Billy Smith	46	0	0	0	11

N.Y. RANGERS

	GP	G	A	Pts	Pim
Brad Park	78	25	57	82	148
Rod Gilbert	75	36	41	77	20
Peter Stemkowski	78	25	45	70	74
Jean Ratelle	68	28	39	67	16
Walt Tkaczuk	71	21	42	63	58
Bill Fairbairn	78	18	44	62	12
Steve Vickers	75	34	24	58	18
Vic Hadfield	77	27	28	55	75
Bobby Rousseau	72	10	41	51	4
Ted Irvine	75	26	20	46	105
Bruce MacGregor	66	17	27	44	6
Gilles Marotte	68	3	28	31	51
Rod Seiling	68	7	23	30	32
Jerry Butler	26	6	10	16	24
Dale Rolfe	48	3	12	15	56
Ron Harris	63	2	12	14	25
Jim Neilson	72	4	7	11	38
Lawrence Sacharuk	23	2	4	6	4
Jack Egers	34	1	4	5	12
Bert Wilson	5	1	1	2	2
Ed Giacomin	56	0	1	1	4

PHILADELPHIA

	GP	G	A	Pts	Pim
Bobby Clarke	77	35	52	87	113
Rick MacLeish	78	32	45	77	42
Bill Barber	75	34	35	69	54
Ross Lonsberry	75	32	19	51	48
Gary Dornhoefer	57	11	39	50	125
Bill Flett	67	17	27	44	51
Orest Kindrachuk	71	11	30	41	85
Don Saleski	77	15	25	40	131
Dave Schultz	73	20	16	36	348
Simon Nolet	52	19	17	36	13
Tom Bladon	70	12	22	34	37
Terry Crisp	71	10	21	31	28
Andre Dupont	75	3	20	23	216
Jimmy Watson	78	2	18	20	44
Ed Van Impe	77	2	16	18	119
Joe Watson	74	1	17	18	34
Bill Clement	39	9	8	17	34
Barry Ashbee	69	4	13	17	52
Bob Kelly	65	4	10	14	130
Bernie Parent	73	0	3	3	24
Serge Lajeunesse	1	0	0	0	0
Al MacAdam	5	0	0	0	0
Bobby Taylor	8	0	0	0	12

PITTSBURGH

	GP	G	A	Pts	Pim
Syl Apps	75	24	61	85	37
Lowell MacDonald	78	43	39	82	14
Jean Pronovost	77	40	32	72	22
Ron Schock	77	14	29	43	22
Ron Stackhouse	69	6	29	35	66
Bob Kelly	67	16	18	34	123
Chuck Arnason	74	20	11	31	17
Ab Demarco	57	10	21	31	15
Ron Lalonde	73	10	17	27	14
Steve Durbano	69	8	19	27	284
Wayne Bianchin	69	12	13	25	38
Bernie Lukowich	53	9	10	19	32
Bob McManama	47	5	14	19	18
Dave Burrows	71	3	14	17	30
Ted Snell	55	4	12	16	8
Nick Beverley	68	2	14	16	21
Blaine Stoughton	34	5	6	11	8
Bob Paradise	56	2	8	10	52
Jean Guy Lagace	31	2	6	8	34
Yvon Labre	16	1	2	3	13
Larry Bignell	20	0	3	3	2
Jim Wiley	22	0	3	3	2
Ron Jones	25	0	3	3	15
Hank Nowak	13	0	0	0	11
Andy Brown	36	0	0	0	60

ST. LOUIS

	GP	G	A	Pts	Pim
Garry Unger	78	33	35	68	96
Pierre Plante	78	26	28	54	85
Greg Polis	78	22	25	47	56
Glen Sather	71	15	29	44	82
Wayne Merrick	64	20	23	43	32
Lou Angotti	51	12	23	35	9
Garnett Bailey	67	16	17	33	53
Floyd Thomson	77	11	22	33	58
Bill Collins	66	15	17	32	51
Gary Sabourin	54	7	23	30	27
Barclay Plager	72	6	20	26	99
Larry Giroux	74	5	17	22	59
Don Awrey	75	5	16	21	51
Nick Harbaruk	56	5	14	19	16
Dave Gardner	46	6	12	18	8
Ted Harris	77	0	16	16	86
John Wright	52	6	9	15	33
Gord Brooks	30	6	8	14	12
Butch Williams	32	3	10	13	6
Bob Plager	61	3	10	13	48
Bob Collyard	10	1	3	4	4
Bob Gassoff	28	0	3	3	84
Phil Roberto	15	1	1	2	10
Wayne Stephenson	38	0	1	1	2
Glenn Patrick	1	0	0	0	2
Frank Spring	2	0	0	0	0
John Wensink	3	0	0	0	0

Connie Forey	4	0	0	0	2
Bernie MacNeil	4	0	0	0	0
John Davidson	39	0	0	0	10

TORONTO

	GP	G	A	Pts	Pim
Darryl Sittler	78	38	46	84	55
Norm Ullman	78	22	47	69	12
Paul Henderson	69	24	31	55	40
Dave Keon	74	25	28	53	7
Ron Ellis	70	23	25	48	12
Inge Hammarstrom	66	20	23	43	14
Jim McKenny	77	14	28	42	36
Rick Kehoe	69	18	22	40	8
Borje Salming	76	5	34	39	48
Ian Turnbull	78	8	27	35	74
Mike Pelyk	71	12	19	31	94
Lanny McDonald	70	14	16	30	43
Tim Ecclestone	60	9	19	28	38
Garry Monahan	78	9	16	25	70
Brian Glennie	65	4	18	22	100
Denis Dupere	34	8	9	17	8
Errol Thompson	56	7	8	15	6
Eddie Shack	59	7	8	15	74
Bob Neely	54	5	7	12	98
George Ferguson	16	0	4	4	4
Willie Brossart	17	0	1	1	20
Dunc Wilson	24	0	0	0	6
Doug Favell	32	0	0	0	20

VANCOUVER

	GP	G	A	Pts	Pim
Andre Boudrias	78	16	59	75	18
Dennis Ververgaert	78	26	31	57	25
Don Lever	78	23	25	48	28
Gerry O'Flaherty	78	22	20	42	18
Jocelyn Guevremont	72	15	24	39	34
Dave Dunn	68	11	22	33	76
Barry Wilkins	78	3	28	31	123
Chris Oddleifson	70	13	16	29	44
John Gould	75	13	12	25	10
Paulin Bordeleau	68	11	13	24	20
Bob Dailey	76	7	17	24	143
Richard Lemieux	72	5	17	22	23
Orland Kurtenbach	52	8	13	21	30
Don Tannahill	33	8	12	20	4
Tracy Pratt	78	3	15	18	96
Dennis Kearns	52	4	13	17	30
Bryan McSheffrey	54	9	3	12	34
Greg Boddy	53	2	10	12	59
Bobby Lalonde	36	3	4	7	18
Jim Mair	6	1	3	4	0
Mike Lampman	29	2	0	2	0
Danny Seguin	1	1	0	1	0
Dennis McCord	1	0	0	0	0
Eugene Sobchuk	1	0	0	0	0

Peter Folco	2	0	0	0	0
Dan Gloor	2	0	0	0	0
Larry Gould	2	0	0	0	0
Dennis McCord	2	0	0	0	6
Steve Stone	2	0	0	0	0
Paul O'Neil	5	0	0	0	0
Jacques Caron	10	0	0	0	2
Gary Smith	66	0	0	0	47

GOALTENDING

		GPI	Mins	GA	EN	SO	Ave	W	L	T
Bernie Parent	Phila.	73	4314	136	2	12	1.89	47	13	12
Bobby Taylor	Phila.	7	366	26	0	0	4.26	3	3	0
Philadelphia	**Totals**	**78**	**4680**	**164**		**12**	**2.10**	**50**	**16**	**12**
Tony Esposito	Chi.	70	4143	141	3	10	2.04	34	14	21
Mike Veisor	Chi.	10	537	20	0	1	2.23	7	0	2
Chicago	**Totals**	**78**	**4680**	**164**		**11**	**2.10**	**41**	**14**	**23**
Ross Brooks	Bos.	21	1170	46	0	3	2.36	16	3	0
Gilles Gilbert	Bost.	54	3210	158	0	6	2.95	34	12	8
Ken Broderick	Bost.	5	300	16	1	0	3.20	2	2	1
Boston	**Totals**	**78**	**4680**	**221**		**9**	**2.83**	**52**	**17**	**9**
Doug Favell	Tor.	32	1752	79	1	0	2.71	14	7	9
Dunc Wilson	Tor.	24	1412	68	3	1	2.89	9	11	3
Ed Johnston	Tor.	26	1516	78	1	1	3.09	12	9	4
Toronto	**Totals**	**78**	**4680**	**230**		**2**	**2.95**	**35**	**27**	**16**
Rogie Vachon	Los Ang.	65	3751	175	5	5	2.80	28	26	10
Gary Edwards	Los Ang.	18	929	50	1	1	3.23	5	7	2
Los Angeles	**Totals**	**78**	**4680**	**231**		**6**	**2.96**	**33**	**33**	**12**
Dan Bouchard	Atl.	46	2660	123	3	5	2.77	19	18	8
Phil Myre	Atl.	36	2020	112	0	0	3.33	11	16	6
Atlanta	**Totals**	**78**	**4680**	**238**		**5**	**3.05**	**30**	**34**	**14**
Wayne Thomas	Mont.	42	2410	111	1	1	2.76	23	12	5
Michel Larocque	Mont.	27	1431	69	2	0	2.89	15	8	2
Michel Plasse	Mont.	15	839	57	0	0	4.08	7	4	2
Montreal	**Totals**	**78**	**4680**	**240**		**1**	**3.08**	**45**	**24**	**9**
Glenn Resch	Islanders	2	120	6	0	0	3.00	1	1	0
Billy Smith	Islanders	46	2615	134	5	0	3.07	9	23	12
Gerry Desjardins	Islanders	36	1945	101	1	0	3.12	9	17	6
N.Y. Islanders	**Totals**	**78**	**4680**	**247**		**0**	**3.17**	**19**	**41**	**18**
John Davidson	St. Lou.	39	2300	118	3	0	3.08	13	19	7
Wayne Stephenson	St. Lou.	40	2360	123	2	2	3.13	13	21	5
Jim Watt	St. Lou.	1	20	2	0	0	6.00	0	0	0
St. Louis	**Totals**	**78**	**4680**	**248**		**2**	**3.18**	**26**	**40**	**12**
Dave Dryden	Buf.	53	2987	148	3	1	2.97	23	20	8
Rocky Farr	Buf.	11	480	25	2	0	3.13	2	4	1
Gary Bromley	Buf.	12	598	33	0	0	3.31	3	5	3
Roger Crozier	Buf.	12	615	39	0	0	3.80	4	5	0
Buffalo	**Totals**	**78**	**4680**	**250**		**1**	**3.21**	**32**	**34**	**12**

Ed Giacomin	Rangers	56	3286	168	1	5	3.07	30	15	10
Peter McDuffe	Rangers	6	340	18	0	0	3.18	3	2	1
Gilles Villemure	Rangers	21	1054	62	2	0	3.53	7	7	3
N.Y. Rangers	**Totals**	**78**	**4680**	**251**		**5**	**3.22**	**40**	**24**	**14**
Gary Inness	Pitts.	20	1032	56	1	0	3.26	7	10	1
Jim Rutherford	Pitts.	26	1432	82	1	0	3.44	7	12	4
Andy Brown	Pitts.	36	1956	115	0	1	3.53	13	16	4
Denis Herron	Pitts.	5	260	18	0	0	4.15	1	3	0
Pittsburgh	**Totals**	**78**	**4680**	**273**		**1**	**3.50**	**28**	**41**	**9**
Gump Worsley	Minn.	29	1601	86	0	0	3.22	8	14	5
Cesare Maniago	Minn.	40	2378	138	0	1	3.48	12	18	10
Fern Rivard	Minn.	13	701	50	1	1	4.28	3	6	2
Minnesota	**Totals**	**78**	**4680**	**275**		**2**	**3.53**	**23**	**38**	**17**
Gary Smith	Van.	65	3632	208	5	3	3.44	20	33	8
Ed Dyck	Van.	12	583	45	0	0	4.63	2	5	2
Jacques Caron	Van.	10	465	38	0	0	4.90	2	5	1
Vancouver	**Totals**	**78**	**4680**	**296**		**3**	**3.79**	**24**	**43**	**11**
Bill McKenzie	Det.	13	720	43	0	1	3.58	4	4	4
Jim Rutherford	Det.	25	1420	86	0	0	3.63	9	11	4
Doug Grant	Det.	37	2018	140	0	1	4.16	15	16	2
Terry Richardson	Det.	9	315	28	0	0	5.33	1	4	0
Roy Edwards	Det.	4	187	18	0	0	5.78	0	3	0
Denis Dejordy	Det.	1	20	4	0	0	12.00	0	1	0
Detroit	**Totals**	**78**	**4680**	**319**		**2**	**4.09**	**29**	**39**	**10**
Ted Tucker	Cal.	5	177	10	0	0	3.39	1	1	1
Marv Edwards	Cal.	14	780	51	0	0	3.92	1	10	1
Gilles Meloche	Cal.	47	2800	198	2	1	4.24	9	33	5
Bob Champoux	Cal.	17	923	80	1	0	5.20	2	11	3
California	**Totals**	**78**	**4680**	**342**		**1**	**4.38**	**13**	**55**	**10**

WHA REVIEW

Dennis Murphy, President of the World Hockey Association, says 1973-74, the league's second year of existence, "was a very difficult one." Indeed, it was.

Hardly anyone in professional sports could admit to having faced as many problems as Murphy did from the time he assumed office early in the season until the playoffs ended mercifully on May 19. Mere weeks after the season ended, three of the 12 franchises had been moved, others battled severe financial problems and the network television contract with CBS had virtually evaporated in front of his eyes.

And it didn't take long for the problems to surface, especially in New York.

No team in recent sports history has been followed by a darker cloud than the New York WHA franchise. Originally named the Raiders at the league's inception, the club managed only a few months of operation before running out of money—forcing the league office to assume control.

The hope was that as the 1973-74 season opened, those troubles would be over. There were new owners (reportedly with big-money backing), new players like Andre Lacroix, the first season's scoring champion, and a new name: the Golden Blades.

But the gold on the blades tarnished very quickly—almost as quickly as the gold ran out in the club's treasury. The new owners couldn't even meet their first payroll of the regular season, and again the league was forced to take over until another sale could take place. New York, which had been the twinkle in the eye of WHA officials, quickly became an embarrassment.

Gordie Howe led Houston to the WHA championship, scoring 100 points for the Aeros.

A second-year league does not take embarrassment lightly. It can't afford that luxury. So, under incredible pressure, the WHA again took control of the club and moved it to Cherry Hill, New Jersey, where the team eventually was purchased by Baltimore-based real estate wizard Joseph Schwartz.

In Cherry Hill, the team acquired its third name, the Knights, played in a dismally inadequate 5,000-seat arena, and, not surprisingly, finished dead last in the East Division. The bath in red ink that resulted forced a third change in a matter of months: The team was moved to San Diego, where Murphy and the other league officials can only hope things will improve.

The move to the West Coast was forced by the departure of the Los Angeles Sharks from the sunny Pacific city. The WHA, already without a major franchise on the East Coast, could not tolerate a similar situation in the west.

The Sharks, owned secretly by Dr. Leonard Bloom (better known for owning Wilt Chamberlain and the American Basketball Association's San Diego Conquistadores), were sold to a Detroit firm and named the Michigan Stags. In a matter of weeks, the cellar-dwellers of both divisions had moved.

The change may do them good.

But what of the New England Whalers, who were forced out of Boston to Hartford, Connecticut? The Whalers, although eliminated in last season's playoff quarter-finals, had won the East Division title for the second consecutive year. They won the first World Cup ever by beating Bobby Hull and the Winnipeg Jets to cap a successful 1972-73 season. What could force them out of their home? Money. Just like New York, but to a lesser degree.

Whalers' president Howard Baldwin, who would later concentrate more heavily on interests in the World Football League, hit the nail right on the head: "Quite candidly, the stockholders of the Whalers have lost considerable sums of money over the past two years in order to make the club a success in Boston."

They didn't want to lose any more.

The dates at New England's Boston Garden home had been disappointing. There was, after all, competition with teams named the Bruins and the Celtics, and when those teams carved out their dates, little could be done to create an attractive schedule out of the remaining dates.

The crowds were disappointing as a result—thus the move to greener pastures.

While all the front-office tumult raged, there was a hockey season going on. The Edmonton Oilers sailed through the first five weeks of the season as though the one game they had lost would be their only setback of the year. Boosted by playing eight of their first nine games at home, the Oilers struck for 11 consecutive victories and breezed to the top of the West Division.

In the East, the Whalers resumed their familiar spot atop the East—a position they would retain virtually throughout the season. At times, the Quebec Nordiques and Toronto Toros would offer mild runs at the top spot, while Cleveland's Crusaders played the steady, careful kind of game that would carry them into the playoffs again. The Chicago Cougars kept their heads above water with a number of new faces, but New York already had begun to sink to the basement spot it would occupy for the second straight year.

Edmonton's Jim Harrison kept the Oiler fire ablaze with eight goals and 19 assists in the first 13 games. John Garrett was the hot goalie at the time, stopping all but 15 of the 240 shots taken at him in his first seven games for the Minnesota Fighting Saints.

The Houston Aeros hadn't really taken off then. In the city where they call a four-goal game "a Texas hat-trick," the Howe family was feeling its way, working into shape, priming itself for the long drive that would lead to the World Cup title.

For Papa Gordie, it would be a while before he could convince his body that retirement was over. He had made his first official appearance as an Aero during an exhibition in New York's Madison Square Garden.

When it was over, Gordie sat in the steamy dressing room and his age showed like an aging movie star's double chin. Long after the not-too-large crowd had departed, Howe took deep breaths in an effort to recapture his wind.

He looked old. More than his 46 years and 25 hockey seasons. And many of the players in the dressing room sat on their benches and just stared at this man, aware that his performance meant the difference in their season.

Not far away sat the two younger Howes, the only hockey players ever to compete with a parent in a professional rink. Mark, the youngest at 18, showed potential—potential that would bring him Rookie of the Year honors. Marty, at 20, indicated he might need more time to adjust to the professional game. But, appropriately, he was more cautious from his position as defenseman than brother Mark had to be at left wing.

"Can you imagine," Mark Howe asked nobody in particular, "how embarrassing it's going to be for me to yell, 'Dad! Dad!' every time I want the puck?"

That may have been true, but Mark overcame his bashfulness in time to score 39 goals and add 41 assists in his first professional season—a total it took his father four years to reach in the National Hockey League. Gordie, meanwhile, overcame the rustiness to total 100 points, his best production ever, and was the WHA's MVP.

That is not to say, however, that the Howes carried the Houston team to the title. Don McLeod finished with the best average among goaltenders, 2.57; right

Ralph Backstrom (left) and player-coach Pat Stapleton boosted the WHA Chicago Cougars to the semifinal playoffs last season.

wing Frank Hughes scored 42 goals—13 on the power play; left wing Andre Hinse led all rookie scorers with 24 goals and 56 assists for 80 points, and a solid defense anchored by Poul Popiel, John Schella, Gordon Kannegeisser and Larry Hale contributed to the team effort.

A similar mixture of all the basic ingredients carried New England home first in the East. Al Smith pulled much of the goaltending duty, and eventually would finish as the WHA's third-leading goaltender with a 3.08 goals against average. The defense, led by Jim Dorey, Ted Green, Brad Selwood and Rick Ley, would combine to allow just 260 goals—second only to Houston's 219—when the season ended. The forward lines produced balanced scoring with John French leading on 72 points.

It is that combination which can produce championships: team efforts, few standouts, and solid goaltending. But there were other teams with less outstanding credentials who made the playoff race exciting to the last day.

The struggle for supremacy, like the rest of this unusual season, bears telling.

Surprisingly, hockey's household name, Bobby Hull, was overshadowed as the year unfolded. The Jets played inconsistently and would manage only a fourth-place finish in the West. A year earlier, they had reached the World Cup finals.

The Hull magic, muted slightly by nagging injuries, remained, however. In the minds of many, on the morning of January 19, he reinforced his image as the all-time great goodwill ambassador of sport.

The night before, an apartment house fire killed nine people and left 16 families homeless in Winnipeg. The next morning at practice, Hull collected $145 in cash from his teammates, along with children's clothes, suits, bedding and other supplies to be given to the troubled families.

In Winnipeg, however, there were grumblings on the

ice. Discipline was a problem with Hull's Jets. One of Hull's former teammates, Lou Angotti, suggested that the cause of the lack of discipline was that Hull had never been disciplined himself. How could a man who had never been controlled turn around and control his mates?

The question, although never answered verbally, showed up in the standings and in the playoffs, during which the Jets were blown out in four games by Houston.

Minnesota's Fighting Saints fared somewhat better, thanks to Mike Walton and a team that proved itself one of the most belligerent in the league. As the season came down the home stretch, Walton got hot and so did his teammates.

During a 16-game rampage, the left wing amassed 26 goals and 17 assists, including back-to-back four-goal games followed by a three-goal game. The Saints, as a result, went on a tear in which they lost only three of 21 and challenged the Aeros for first place in the West. Walton finished as the WHA scoring champion with 117 points, including 57 goals.

By the All-Star break, the Edmonton Oilers began to slip. Their earlier skein of victories proved itself a peak that came far too early to be of any help as the season continued. The points provided in those first weeks, however, provided them with enough of a bulge to hold off Winnipeg for third place in the West.

Vancouver, although drawing well at the Pacific Coliseum home it shared with the National Hockey League Canucks, fell far behind the leaders and never caught up. Danny Lawson, the right wing who led the league in goals with 61 the year before, scored 50 for the Blazers in 1973-74 but couldn't carry the Blazers' offense alone.

Veteran Bryan Campbell tied Lawson for the club's point-scoring lead with 88, but it was 20 points ahead of No. 3 scorer Claude St. Sauveur, a rookie.

In Los Angeles, things were worse. Only three teams actually drew less at home in the second season than they did in the first, and Los Angeles was one of them (the Whalers and the Golden Blades-Knights were the others). The Sharks scored just 239 goals—20 less than in their opening season, while their goals-against ballooned from a solid 250 to an embarrassing 339—better only than Vancouver.

Marc Tardif, who jumped from the Montreal Canadiens to Los Angeles before the season began, led the Sharks with 70 points, with veteran Gary Veneruzzo second at 68.

On the whole, the East Division race provided far more suspense. The struggle for playoff spots was very similar to the one that had marked the WHA's opening season.

For the Whalers, of course, there was little worry about a second division title. But the battle behind them was hard-fought indeed.

As the season closed, the first -and fifth-place teams were separated by just 10 points (the second through fifth teams were a mere six points apart). The biggest surprise came from the Chicago Cougars. The Cougars had finished last in the West Division in 1972-73, but had shifted to the East during the off season when Philadelphia was transferred to Vancouver. Meanwhile, standout defenseman Pat Stapleton had been lured from the Chicago Black Hawks of the NHL, as had veteran center Ralph Backstrom. Cam Newton left the Pittsburgh Penguins to play goal for the Cougars while a force of little-known players carried the team to fourth place and the playoffs.

It is doubtful that the Cougars expected to reach the World Cup final against the Aeros, with defending champion New England cruising into the playoffs and the Cougars having been forced out of their arena by a production of Peter Pan.

Somehow, they managed. But not without a struggle.

Winnipeg goalie Ernie Wakely makes the save on New England's John French.

Jets
FRENCH
11

Except for the Jersey Knights, who suffered too long from inner turmoil and the troubles of relocating in New Jersey, everybody had a chance at the playoffs. The Toronto Toros, moved from Ottawa before the season started, sprinted into second place with 86 points.

The Toros, paced by goaltender Gilles Gratton and left wing Wayne "Swoop" Carleton, showed strength in early December when they won six of eight games although five regulars were out with injuries and two were playing hurt. They once scored eight goals in the final period of a 10-1 triumph over Minnesota. Around that time Carleton was leading the league in scoring, although he finished sixth in the race with 92 points.

Cleveland was paced by Gerry Cheevers. They surmounted a 10-24-5 record on the road to finish third with 83 points. Cheevers led the league in shutouts with four, and led in shutout periods with 73, but finished second to Houston's McLeod with a 3.03 goals-against average.

The Crusaders had a good-looking rookie in Tom Edur, but it was the veterans who carried the club to third place. Gary Jarrett led the team in scoring with 71 points, followed by Ron Ward's 61. Ward set an unusual WHA record, scoring three hat tricks for three teams in one season. The league's second leading scorer while with the old New York Raiders in 1972-73, Ward had started last season with Vancouver, had been traded to Los Angeles and then to Cleveland.

Otherwise, it was veterans—Jim Wiste, Gerry Pinder, Skip Krake and especially Paul Schmyr, who has acquired the reputation as the WHA's outstanding defenseman—that carried Cleveland.

Not far behind lurked the Cougars at 81 points. They edged the Quebec Nordiques by a point for the final playoff berth, then started their surprising climb to the finals with a seven-game victory over the displaced Whalers.

Then came a tooth-and-nail seven-game triumph over the Toros, although the Cougars were forced to play in a 3,000-seat rink in a suburban shopping center because their original home had made a previous commitment. The Toros suffered from a similar fate during the playoffs, for their regular season home, Toronto's Varsity Arena, was converted into an examination hall as the University's semester came to a close.

Toronto got the better home ice of the two, though. Toros' owner John Bassett and Maple Leafs' owner Harold Ballard settled a long-standing family feud, and the Toros gained use of historic Maple Leaf Gardens for the playoffs.

It did them little good in the seventh game of the series, for the Cougars clawed for four second-period goals to wipe out an early deficit . . . and the Toros.

Meanwhile, the Aeros swept past Winnipeg in four games, including a 10-1 rout in game three. Coupled with the Whalers' loss to the Cougars, last year's World Cup finalists found themselves also-rans.

Minnesota dispatched Edmonton in five games, then lost to the Houston Howes in the second round. Toronto had ousted Cheevers and Cleveland 4-1 in their first-round set, but met up with the hungry Cougars in the semis.

So the stage was set. Underdog Chicago and confident Houston met in the finals. But the series was strictly no contest. The Aeros used the Howes and a potent power play to sweep past Chicago in four games and win the city's first pro sports title since the Houston Oilers took the American Football League crown in 1961.

At center ice in Sam Houston Coliseum, Dennis Murphy presented the World Cup to the Aeros, and the year of crisis was finally over.

1973-74 WHA STANDINGS AND STATISTICS

EASTERN DIVISION

	GP	W	L	T	PTS	GF	GA
New England	78	43	31	4	90	291	260
Toronto	78	41	33	4	86	304	272
Cleveland	78	37	32	9	83	266	264
Chicago	78	38	35	5	81	271	273
Quebec	78	38	36	4	80	306	280
New Jersey	78	32	42	4	68	268	313

WESTERN DIVISION

	GP	W	L	T	PTS	GF	GA
Houston	78	48	25	5	101	318	219
Minnesota	78	44	32	2	90	332	275
Edmonton	78	38	37	3	79	268	269
Winnipeg	78	34	39	5	73	264	296
Vancouver	78	27	50	1	55	278	345
Los Angeles	78	25	53	0	50	239	339

INDIVIDUAL SCORING LEADERS

Player & Team	GP	G	A	PTS	PIM
Mike Walton, Minnesota	78	57	60	117	88
Andre Lacroix, New Jersey	78	31	80	111	54
Gordie Howe, Houston	70	31	69	100	46
Bobby Hull, Winnipeg	75	53	42	95	38
Wayne Connelly, Minnesota	78	42	53	95	16
Wayne Carleton, Toronto	78	37	55	92	31
Danny Lawson, Vancouver	78	50	38	88	14
Bryan Campbell, Vancouver	76	27	61	88	48
Serge Bernier, Quebec	74	37	49	86	107
Larry Lund, Houston	75	33	53	86	109
Frank Hughes, Houston	74	42	42	84	47
Ralph Backstrom, Chicago	78	33	50	83	26
Andre Hinse, Houston	69	24	56	80	39
Mark Howe, Houston	76	38	41	79	20
George Morrison, Minnesota	73	40	38	78	37
Chris Bordeleau, Winnipeg	75	26	49	75	22
Ron Climie, Edmonton	75	38	36	74	22
Fran Huck, Winnipeg	74	26	48	74	69
Rosaire Paiement, Chicago	78	30	43	73	87
John French, New England	77	24	48	72	31
Gary Jarrett, Cleveland	75	31	40	71	70
Marc Tardif, Los Angeles	75	40	30	70	47
Tom Webster, New England	64	43	26	69	28
Larry Pleau, New England	77	26	43	69	35
Jim Harrison, Edmonton	47	24	45	69	99
Gary Veneruzzo, Los Angeles	78	39	29	68	68
Claude St. Sauveur, Vancouver	70	38	30	68	55
Robert Guindon, Quebec	77	31	37	68	30
Andre Gaudette, Quebec	78	24	44	68	16
Gavin Kirk, Toronto	78	20	48	68	44

CHICAGO

	GP	G	A	PTS	PIM
Ralph Backstrom	78	33	50	83	26
Rosaire Paiement	78	30	43	73	87
Joe Hardy	77	24	35	59	55
Pat Stapleton	78	6	52	58	44
Larry Mavety	77	15	35	50	157
Bob Liddington	73	26	21	47	20
Bobby Sicinski	69	11	29	40	8
Jan Popiel	63	22	16	38	36
Rick Morris	76	17	16	33	140
Duke Harris	64	14	16	30	20
Darryl Maggs	78	8	22	30	146
Don Gordon	52	13	10	23	33
Frankie Rochon	69	12	11	23	27
Dick Proceviat	77	2	20	22	55
Rod Zaine	77	5	13	18	17
Reg Fleming	45	2	12	14	49
Brian Coates	50	10	3	13	14
Jim Benzelock	53	5	7	12	19
Jim Watson	71	0	11	11	50
Eric Nesterenko	29	2	5	7	8
Brian Glenwright	15	3	2	5	0
John Shmyr	43	1	3	4	13
Lorne Rombough	3	1	2	3	0
Curt Brackenbury	4	0	1	1	11
Gary Connelly	4	0	1	1	2
Dave Walter	4	0	1	1	0
Cam Newton	47	0	1	1	0
Jim Jones	1	0	0	0	0
Ron Anderson	2	0	0	0	0
Al MacKenzie	2	0	0	0	0
Larry Cahan	3	0	0	0	2
Andre Gill	13	0	0	0	0
Rich Coutu	20	0	0	0	0

Goaltenders	**MIN**	**GP**	**W**	**L**	**T**	**Pct.**	**GA**	**Avg.**	**EN**	**SH**
Cam Newton	2732	45	25	18	2	.578	142	3.12	4	1
Andre Gill	803	13	4	7	2	.385	46	3.44	1	0
Rich Coutu	1207	20	9	10	1	.475	75	3.73	3	0
Totals	**4742**	**78**	**38**	**35**	**5**	**.519**	**263**	**3.33**	**9**	**1**

CLEVELAND

	GP	G	A	PTS	PIM
Gary Jarrett	75	31	40	71	71
Ron Ward	70	33	28	61	25
Jim Wiste	76	23	35	58	24
Gerry Pinder	76	23	33	56	90
Skip Krake	69	20	36	56	94
Grant Erickson	78	23	27	50	26
Ron Buchanan	49	18	28	46	2
Paul Shmyr	78	12	31	43	165
Ray Clearwater	68	12	23	35	47
Tom Edur	76	7	31	38	26
Paul Andrea	69	15	18	33	14
Russ Walker	76	15	13	28	117
Larry Hillman	44	5	21	26	37
Doug Brindley	30	13	9	22	13
Billy Heindl	67	4	14	18	4
Rob Neale	43	8	9	17	30
Wayne Muloin	76	3	7	10	39

Wayne Hillman	66	1	7	8	51
Norm Cournoyer	14	3	5	8	6
Dick Pumple	17	2	2	4	16
Ron Morgan	4	0	1	1	7
Bob Whidden	22	0	1	1	2
Ray Adduono	2	0	0	0	0
Glen Shirton	4	0	0	0	0
Jim McMasters	9	0	0	0	4
Brad Buetow	25	0	0	0	4
Gerry Cheevers	61	0	0	0	30

Goaltenders	**MIN**	**GP**	**W**	**L**	**T**	**Pct.**	**GA**	**Avg.**	**EN**	**SH**
Gerry Cheevers	3562	59	30	20	6	.589	180	3.03	4	4
Bob Whidden	1232	22	7	12	3	.386	80	3.90	0	1
Totals	**4793**	**78**	**37**	**32**	**9**	**.532**	**260**	**3.26**	**4**	**5**

EDMONTON

	GP	**G**	**A**	**PTS**	**PIM**
Ron Climie	75	38	36	74	22
Jim Harrison	47	24	45	69	99
Al Hamilton	78	14	45	59	104
Ross Perkins	78	16	40	56	43
Len Lunde	72	26	22	48	8
Blair McDonald	78	21	24	45	34
Rusty Patenaude	71	20	23	43	58
Tom Gilmore	57	19	23	42	164
Brian McKenzie	78	18	20	38	66
Bob Wall	76	6	30	36	46
Ken Baird	69	17	19	36	117
Doug Barrie	70	4	27	31	214
Bobby Sheehan	59	13	11	24	14
Bob McAneeley	41	12	11	23	49
Val Fonteyne	72	9	13	22	2
Eddie Joyal	45	8	10	18	2
Bob Falkenberg	77	3	14	17	32
Steve Carlyle	53	2	13	15	18
Ron Anderson	18	5	2	7	4
Jim McCrimmon	68	2	3	5	106
Bob Fitchner	31	1	2	3	23
Jack Norris	53	0	3	3	0
Roger Cote	56	0	3	3	34
Jim Schraefel	33	1	1	2	0
Brian Carlin	5	1	0	1	0
Gary Doyle	1	0	0	0	0
Hal Colborne	2	0	0	0	0
Gary Cunningham	2	0	0	0	0
Ian Wilkie	28	0	0	0	2
Chris Worthy	30	0	0	0	13

Goaltenders	**MIN**	**GP**	**W**	**L**	**T**	**Pct.**	**GA**	**Avg.**	**EN**	**SH**
Jack Norris	2954	53	23	24	1	.490	158	3.21	5	2
Ian Wilkie										
Edmonton Totals	256	5	3	1	1	.700	9	2.11	0	0
Season Totals	1514	28	14	10	1	.580	91	3.61	0	1
Chris Worthy	1453	29	11	12	1	.479	92	3.80	1	1
Gary Doyle	60	1	1	0	0	1.000	4	4.00	0	0
Totals	**4723**	**78**	**38**	**37**	**3**	**.506**	**262**	**3.33**	**6**	**3**

HOUSTON

	GP	**G**	**A**	**PTS**	**PIM**
Gordie Howe	70	31	69	100	46

	GP	G	A	PTS	PIM
Larry Lund	75	33	53	86	109
Frank Hughes	74	42	42	84	47
Andre Hinse	69	24	56	80	39
Mark Howe	76	38	41	79	20
Jim Sherritt	76	30	28	58	18
Murray Hall	78	29	29	58	25
Gordon Labossiere	67	19	36	55	30
Poul Popiel	78	7	41	48	120
Ted Taylor	75	23	23	44	143
John Schella	73	12	19	31	170
Don Grierson	65	11	18	29	45
Marty Howe	73	4	20	24	90
Gordon Kannegeisser	78	0	20	20	26
Joe Szura	42	8	7	15	4
Larry Hale	69	2	13	15	39
Gary Williamson	9	2	6	8	0
Jack Stanfield	42	1	3	4	2
Bill Prentice	55	1	2	3	35
Don McLeod	51	0	3	3	6
Ed Hoekstra	19	2	0	2	0
Wayne Rutledge	27	0	1	1	14
Don Grahame	4	0	0	0	0

Goaltenders	**MIN**	**GP**	**W**	**L**	**T**	**Pct.**	**GA**	**Avg.**	**EN**	**SH**
Ron Grahame	250	4	3	0	1	.875	5	1.20	0	1
Don McLeod	2971	49	33	13	3	.704	127	2.56	3	3
Wayne Rutledge	1509	25	12	12	1	.500	84	3.34	0	0
Totals	**4730**	**78**	**48**	**25**	**5**	**.647**	**216**	**2.74**	**3**	**4**

LOS ANGELES

	GP	G	A	PTS	PIM
Marc Tardif	75	40	30	70	47
Gary Veneruzzo	78	39	29	68	68
J.P. LeBlanc	78	20	46	66	58
Brian McDonald	56	22	30	52	56
Bobby Whitlock	66	20	29	49	30
Gerry Odrowski	77	4	32	36	48
Reg Thomas	72	14	21	35	22
Steve Sutherland	72	20	12	32	182
Bart Crashley	78	4	26	30	16
Ron Walters	71	14	14	28	30
Bill Young	69	9	12	21	74
Alton White	48	8	13	21	11
Tommy Serviss	74	6	15	21	39
Jim Niekamp	76	2	19	21	95
Ron Garwasiuk	51	6	13	19	100
Ted Hodgson	33	3	11	14	22
Jerry Zrymiak	27	2	8	10	8
Bill Horton	60	0	9	9	46
Fred Speck	18	2	5	7	4
Earl Heiskala	24	2	6	8	45
Ted McCaskill	18	2	2	4	68
Hal Willis	18	1	2	3	24
Peter Slater	19	1	1	2	2
Kirk Bowman	10	0	2	2	0
Mike Hyndman	8	0	1	1	0
Brian Derkson	1	0	0	0	2
Paul Hoganson	27	0	0	0	0
Jimmy McLeod	29	0	0	0	2

Goaltenders	**MIN**	**GP**	**W**	**L**	**T**	**Pct.**	**GA**	**Avg.**	**EN**	**SH**
Paul Hoganson	1308	26	6	16	0	.273	102	4.68	2	0

	MIN	GP	W	L	T	Pct.	GA	Avg.	EN	SH
Jim McLeod	1485	27	7	20	0	.259	105	4.24	1	1
Totals	**4693**	**78**	**25**	**53**	**0**	**.321**	**335**	**4.28**	**4**	**3**

MINNESOTA

	GP	G	A	PTS	PIM
Mike Walton	78	57	60	117	88
Wayne Connelly	78	42	53	95	16
George Morrison	73	40	38	78	37
Murray Heatley	71	26	32	58	23
Ted Hampson	77	17	38	55	9
Jim Johnson	71	15	39	54	30
Mike Antonovich	68	21	29	50	4
John Arbour	77	6	43	49	192
Bob MacMillan	78	14	34	48	81
Steve Cardwell	77	23	23	46	100
Mike McMahon	71	10	35	45	82
Rick Smith	71	10	28	38	98
Keith Christiansen	74	11	25	36	36
Terry Ball	71	8	28	36	34
Gordon Gallant	72	7	15	22	223
Billy Klatt	65	14	6	20	12
Bob Boyd	41	1	14	15	14
Dick Paradise	67	2	7	9	71
Jack McCartan	2	0	0	0	0
Blaine Rydman	8	0	0	0	21
Mike Curran	41	0	0	0	6
John Garrett	42	0	0	0	0

Goaltenders	**MIN**	**GP**	**W**	**L**	**T**	**Pct.**	**GA**	**Avg.**	**EN**	**SH**
Mike Curran	2382	40	23	14	2	.615	130	3.27	2	2
John Garrett	2290	40	21	18	0	.538	137	3.59	1	1
Jack McCartan	42	2	0	0	0	.000	5	7.14	0	0
Totals	**4705**	**78**	**44**	**32**	**2**	**.577**	**272**	**3.47**	**3**	**3**

NEW ENGLAND

	GP	G	A	PTS	PIM
John French	77	24	48	72	31
Tom Webster	64	43	26	69	28
Larry Pleau	77	26	43	69	35
Al Karlander	77	20	40	60	46
Don Blackburn	75	20	39	59	18
Tim Sheehy	77	29	29	58	20
Tommy Williams	70	21	37	58	6
Hugh Harris	75	24	28	52	78
Mike Byers	78	29	21	50	6
Jim Dorey	77	6	39	45	134
Rick Ley	72	6	35	41	148
Brad Selwood	76	9	29	38	91
Ted Green	75	7	26	33	42
Tom Earl	78	10	9	19	29
Paul Hurley	52	3	11	14	21
John Cunniff	30	7	5	12	14
Bob Charlebois	74	4	8	12	6
Guy Smith	16	1	5	6	25
John Danby	72	2	2	4	6
Ric Jordan	34	0	3	3	14
Al Smith	56	0	3	3	33
Mike Keeler	1	0	0	0	0
Bruce Landon	24	0	0	0	24
Bill Berglund	3	0	0	0	0

Goaltenders	MIN	GP	W	L	T	Pct.	GA	Avg.	EN	SH
Al Smith	3194	55	30	21	2	.585	164	3.08	4	2
Bill Berglund	180	3	2	1	0	.667	10	3.33	0	0
Bruce Landon	1386	24	11	9	2	.545	82	3.55	0	0
Totals	**4759**	**78**	**43**	**31**	**4**	**.577**	**256**	**3.23**	**4**	**2**

NEW JERSEY

	GP	G	A	PTS	PIM
Andre Lacroix	78	31	80	111	54
Kevin Morrison	78	23	43	67	132
Wayne Rivers	73	30	26	56	20
Gene Peacosh	68	21	32	53	17
Brian Morenz	75	20	30	50	44
Ken Block	74	3	43	46	22
Bob Jones	78	17	28	45	20
Brian Bradley	78	15	23	38	12
Mike Laughton	71	20	17	37	34
Norm Ferguson	75	15	21	36	12
Don Herriman	44	11	21	32	59
Brian Perry	71	20	11	31	19
Harry Howell	65	3	23	26	24
Bob Brown	59	7	13	20	38
Craig Reichmuth	72	10	8	18	114
Gary Peters	34	2	5	7	18
Ted Scharf	63	4	2	6	107
Dean Boylan	61	1	5	6	112
Bill Speer	66	1	3	4	30
Bob Winograd	7	1	0	1	0
Ray Larose	18	0	1	1	20
Gary Kurt	21	0	1	1	0
Joe Junkin	52	0	1	1	7
Butch Barber	3	0	0	0	2
Claude Chartre	5	0	0	0	0
Lee Inglis	5	0	0	0	0

Goaltenders	MIN	GP	W	L	T	Pct.	GA	Avg.	EN	SH
Joe Junkin	3121	53	21	25	4	.460	197	3.79	3	1
Gary Kurt	1079	20	8	10	0	.444	75	4.17	1	0
Jim McLeod	516	10	3	7	0	.300	36	4.18	1	0
Totals	**4728**	**78**	**32**	**42**	**4**	**.436**	**308**	**3.91**	**5**	**1**

QUEBEC

	GP	G	A	PTS	PIM
Serge Bernier	74	37	49	86	107
Robert Guindon	77	31	37	68	30
Andre Gaudette	78	24	44	68	16
Rejean Houle	66	27	35	62	17
Michel Parizeau	78	26	34	60	41
Jeannot Gilbert	73	17	39	56	20
J.C. Tremblay	68	9	44	53	10
Guy Dufour	75	27	23	50	30
Alain Caron	57	31	15	46	10
Renald Leclerc	53	17	27	44	84
Dale Hoganson	62	8	33	41	27
Alain Beaule	78	4	35	39	93
Francois Lacombe	71	9	27	36	41
Pierre Guite	68	14	20	34	106
Jean-Guy Gendron	64	11	8	19	42
Jean Payette	36	4	12	16	6
Rejean Giroux	12	5	6	11	14
Ken Desjardine	69	2	9	11	46

	GP	G	A	PTS	PIM
Pierre Roy	44	2	7	9	137
Norm Descoteaux	27	1	6	7	6
Mike Rouleau	4	0	3	3	2
Serge Aubry	26	0	1	1	8
Richard Brodeur	30	0	1	1	0
Michel Deguise	32	0	1	1	0
Dave Balon	9	0	0	0	2

Goaltenders	MIN	GP	W	L	T	Pct.	GA	Avg.	EN	SH
Serge Aubry	1395	26	11	11	2	.500	92	3.96	1	1
Michel Deguise	1750	32	12	13	1	.481	96	3.29	1	1
Richard Brodeur	1607	30	14	13	1	.518	89	3.32	3	1
Totals	**4749**	**78**	**38**	**36**	**4**	**.513**	**275**	**3.47**	**5**	**3**

TORONTO

	GP	G	A	PTS	PIM
Wayne Carleton	78	37	55	92	31
Gavin Kirk	78	20	48	68	44
Wayne Dillon	72	39	35	65	13
Guy Trottier	73	26	35	61	63
Rick Sentes	65	26	34	60	46
Tom Martin	75	25	33	58	14
Pat Hickey	78	26	29	55	52
Tom Simpson	73	33	20	53	27
Bob Leduc	61	22	31	53	29
Brian Gibbons	69	4	32	36	84
Steve King	67	13	21	34	26
Brit Selby	63	9	17	26	21
Jack Gibson	65	16	9	25	60
Carl Brewer	77	2	23	25	42
Steve Cuddie	75	5	18	23	65
Rick Cunningham	75	2	18	20	88
Billy Orr	44	3	9	12	14
Mike Amodeo	77	1	11	12	80
Gerry Gibbons	26	1	4	5	23
Peter Marrin	35	1	4	5	4
Lou Nistico	14	1	3	4	14
Gilles Gratton	59	0	4	4	28
William Holden	1	0	0	0	0
Richard Dupras	2	0	0	0	0
Frank Blum	5	0	0	0	0
Les Binkley	25	0	0	0	0

Goaltenders	MIN	GP	W	L	T	Pct.	GA	Avg.	EN	SH
Bill Holden	10	1	0	0	0	.000	0	0.00	0	0
Frank Blum	131	5	1	0	0	1.000	5	2.29	0	0
Les Binkley	1401	27	14	9	1	.604	77	3.30	1	*2
Gilles Gratton	3200	57	26	24	3	.519	188	3.53	1	*1
Totals	**4750**	**78**	**41**	**33**	**4**	**.551**	**270**	**3.41**	**2**	**4**

*—split shutout in Los Angeles, October 16, 1973.

VANCOUVER

	GP	G	A	PTS	PIM
Danny Lawson	78	50	38	88	14
Bryan Campbell	76	27	61	88	48
Claude St. Sauveur	70	38	30	68	55
Don Burgess	78	30	36	66	8
Rob Walton					
Vancouver Totals	28	8	15	23	2
Season Totals	72	16	38	54	26

John McKenzie	45	14	38	52	71
John Migneault	74	21	26	47	27
Murray Meyers	61	22	20	42	28
Ron Plumb	75	6	32	38	40
Jim Adair	70	12	17	29	18
Colin Campbell	78	3	20	23	193
Ralph MacSweyn	72	2	21	23	56
Jim Cardiff	78	1	21	22	188
Mike Chernoff	36	11	10	21	4
Dennis Meloche	41	6	13	19	18
Ed Hatoum	37	3	12	15	8
Don O'Donoghue	49	8	5	13	20
Serge Beaudoin	26	1	11	12	40
Dave Hutchinson	69	0	12	12	151
Sam Gellard	23	7	4	11	15
Jimmy Jones	18	3	2	5	23
Michel Plante	22	3	2	5	2
Camille Lapierre	9	0	3	3	0
Michel Boudreau	3	1	0	1	0
Irvin Spencer	19	0	1	1	6
Peter Donnelly	52	0	1	1	9
Peter McNamee	3	0	0	0	0
Yves Archambault	5	0	0	0	0
Rychard Campeau	7	0	0	0	2
George Gardner	30	0	0	0	0

Goaltenders	**MIN**	**GP**	**W**	**L**	**T**	**Pct.**	**GA**	**Avg.**	**EN**	**SH**
Peter Donnelly	2824	49	22	24	0	.478	180	3.82	3	3
George Gardner	1710	30	4	30	1	.161	138	4.84	3	0
Yves Archambault	263	5	1	4	0	.200	27	6.14	0	0
Danny Sullivan	60	1	0	1	0	.000	7	7.00	0	0
Totals	**4739**	**78**	**27**	**50**	**1**	**.353**	**338**	**4.28**	**7**	**3**

WINNIPEG

	GP	**G**	**A**	**PTS**	**PIM**
Bobby Hull	75	53	42	95	38
Chris Bordeleau	75	26	49	75	22
Fran Huck	74	26	48	74	69
Norm Beaudin	76	27	28	55	8
Ron Snell	70	24	25	49	32
Danny Johnson	78	16	21	37	20
Bob Woytowich	72	6	28	34	43
Jean-Guy Gratton	68	12	21	33	13
Ab McDonald	71	12	17	29	8
Joe Zanussi	76	3	22	25	53
Dan Spring	65	8	16	24	8
Larry Hornung	53	4	19	23	18
Bob Ash	61	2	18	20	30
Ted Hargreaves	74	7	12	19	15
Duke Asmundson	72	5	14	19	85
Dunc Rousseau	61	10	8	18	39
Milt Black	44	6	9	15	14
Bill Sutherland	12	4	5	9	6
Kelly Pratt	50	4	6	10	50
Cal Swenson	26	5	4	9	2
Garth Rizzuto	41	3	4	7	8
Ken Stephenson	29	0	7	7	24
Jim Hargreaves	54	1	4	5	50
Joe Daley	42	0	1	1	4
Bill Holden	1	0	0	0	0
Ernie Wakely	37	0	0	0	9

Goaltenders	MIN	GP	W	L	T	Pct.	GA	Avg.	EN	SH
Ernie Wakely	2254	37	15	18	4	.459	123	3.27	2	3
Bill Holden										
Winnipeg Totals	60	1	0	1	0	.000	4	4.00	0	0
Season Totals	70	2	0	1	0	.000	4	3.43	0	0
Joe Daley	2454	41	19	20	1	.488	163	3.99	4	0
Totals	**4768**	**78**	**34**	**39**	**5**	**.468**	**290**	**3.65**	**6**	**3**

ALL STAR GAMES

NHL ALL STAR GAME

The National Hockey League's West Division, often the subject of ridicule because it is composed of seven expansion teams and the Chicago Black Hawks, got even with the establishment in the annual All Star Game.

After spotting the East a two-goal lead on first period scores by Montreal teammates Frank Mahovlich and Yvan Cournoyer, the West stormed from behind for a 6-4 victory. Bob Berry and Al McDonough tied the game with second period goals and then Lowell MacDonald put the West in front with only 53 seconds left in the middle period.

Stan Mikita and Garry Unger upped the West lead to 5-2 before the East staged a brief comeback on goals by Denis Potvin, the only rookie in the game, and Mickey Redmond. But Pit Martin put a lock on it, scoring the game's final goal with 47 seconds left to play.

Mikita had a goal and two assists, but Unger, whose shorthanded goal was the game-winner, was voted the game's MVP.

The summary:

First period—1, East, F. Mahovlich (Cournoyer, Ullman) 3:33. 2, East, Cournoyer (Ullman) 16:20.

Second period—3, West, Berry (Mikita) 5:59. 4, West, McDonough (Clarke, MacDonald) 13:55. 5, West, MacDonald (B. Plager, Awrey) 19:07.

Third period—West, Mikita (Unger, White) 2:25. 7, West, Unger (White, Mikita) 7:54. 8, East, D. Potvin (unassisted) 9:55. 9, East, M. Redmond (Berenson) 14:55. 10, West, P. Martin (Pappin) 19:13.

WHA ALL STAR GAME

Andre Lacroix wasn't even selected for the East Division team in the World Hockey Association's first All Star Game two years ago, but he enjoyed a strong second half and won the WHA scoring title.

Last season, Lacroix wasn't snubbed. He was in the lineup and made his presence felt with two goals and an assist in the East's 8-4 victory. Larry Pleau also scored twice for the East.

Three of the West goals were scored by Mike Walton, who celebrated his 29th birthday in fine style.

The East packed five goals in the opening period with Lacroix scoring one and setting up another. The West never quite recovered from that early scoring barrage.

Besides Lacroix and Pleau, Rejean Houle, Ralph Backstrom, Gerry Pinder and Rosaire Paiement scored goals for the East. Larry Lund had the only West goal that Walton didn't score.

The summary:

First period—1, East, Houle (Bernier, Paiement) 2:11. 2, East, Backstrom (Carleton, Stapleton) 8:02. 3, East, Pleau (Houle, Paiement) 10:39. 4, West, M. Walton (Lawson) 14:55. 5, East, Pinder (Lacroix, Shmyr) 18:38. 6, East, Lacroix (Jarrett, Pinder) 19:12.

Second period—7, West, M. Walton (Hull, Tardif) 7:27. 8, East, Paiement (Backstrom) 9:15. 9, West, M. Walton (Hamilton, Climie) 16:04. 10, West, Lund (Hamilton, Hughes) 17:28.

Third period—11, East, Lacroix (Jarrett, Pinder) 9:17. 12, East, Pleau (Harris, Webster) 18:59.

THE CUPS

Hockey's regular season is 78 games long, and there are those who will tell you that the teams who finish first after a season-long grind like that are the game's best. They are not, however, the teams remembered afterwards.

That's because the playoffs—hockey's second season—boils down the top teams in the two leagues, eliminating them one by one until finally only one club is left in each league—an NHL champion and a WHA champion. And tradition calls for the league leader to drink champagne out of the championship trophy. In the National Hockey League, that trophy is the historic Stanley Cup. In the World Hockey Association, it is the younger but also cherished World Trophy.

The two trophies look quite similar—bowl-shaped structures sitting atop handsome pedestals. But the NHL's Stanley Cup has had many more adventures than its youthful counterpart.

Lord Stanley's handsome mug, purchased for a mere $48.67 in 1893, has been fiercely contested for and, once won, often has been strangely ignored. It has survived brutal treatment by some of its winners, including the Ottawa Silver Seven. On the way home from a victory celebration, the slightly inebriated Silver Seven found the way to Rideau Canal, where one of the players placekicked the trophy as neatly as a pro football kicker might have. The next day, the hung-over player returned to Rideau, which luckily had been frozen. Sure enough, there was the Stanley Cup.

Another time, members of Montreal's championship team posed proudly with their award in the front room of a photographer. When the picture-taking was over, the players departed, leaving the Cup behind. The photographer's mother discovered it and decided the silverware would make a lovely flowerpot. And it did until somebody rescued it again. The Cup has been swiped by overzealous fans a couple of times—once in the midst of the 1962 playoffs when Chicago's defending champions were wiping out Montreal. A fan wearing a Canadiens' jacket broke into the case in which the Cup was displayed in the lobby of Chicago Stadium and walked off with it. When a guard asked where the fan was going, he explained, "I'm taking the Cup back to Montreal where it belongs."

Episodes like that led the NHL to preserve the Cup permanently in the Hockey Hall of Fame in Toronto. The one presented to playoff champions now is a duplicate, copied in every detail down to the nicks and scratches, but more durable than the elderly original.

Although younger, the WHA's World Trophy has also undergone some curious mishaps. Last spring, when Houston was one victory away from clinching the trophy, WHA officials arranged to have the award shipped to the Texas city. It was supposed to arrive on a Friday for possible presentation Sunday, should the Aeros win a fourth game. When it had not arrived by Saturday, league officials became alarmed.

Eventually, the trophy was located in the office of a parcel delivery company. The office was closed on Sunday and only some telephonic persuasion convinced a janitor to open the door. A league official discovered the 73-pound trophy packed in a cardboard box, and broken. Only three hours before it was presented, a hastily-summoned silversmith patched the trophy together, and the Aeros had tangible evidence of their playoff victory.

NHL STANLEY CUP WINNERS

Season	Champions	Manager	Coach
1973-74	Philadelphia Flyers	Keith Allen	Fred Shero
1972-73	Montreal Canadiens	Sam Pollock	Scotty Bowman
1971-72	Boston Bruins	Milt Schmidt	Tom Johnson
1970-71	Montreal Canadiens	Sam Pollock	Al MacNeil
1969-70	Boston Bruins	Milt Schmidt	Harry Sinden
1968-69	Montreal Canadiens	Sam Pollock	Claude Ruel
1967-68	Montreal Canadiens	Sam Pollock	Toe Blake
1966-67	Toronto Maple Leafs	Punch Imlach	Punch Imlach
1965-66	Montreal Canadiens	Sam Pollock	Toe Blake
1964-65	Montreal Canadiens	Sam Pollock	Toe Blake
1963-64	Toronto Maple Leafs	Punch Imlach	Punch Imlach
1962-63	Toronto Maple Leafs	Punch Imlach	Punch Imlach
1961-62	Toronto Maple Leafs	Punch Imlach	Punch Imlach
1960-61	Chicago Black Hawks	Tommy Ivan	Rudy Pilous
1959-60	Montreal Canadiens	Frank Selke	Toe Blake
1958-59	Montreal Canadiens	Frank Selke	Toe Blake
1957-58	Montreal Canadiens	Frank Selke	Toe Blake
1956-57	Montreal Canadiens	Frank Selke	Toe Blake
1955-56	Montreal Canadiens	Frank Selke	Toe Blake
1954-55	Detroit Red Wings	Jack Adams	Jimmy Skinner
1953-54	Detroit Red Wings	Jack Adams	Tommy Ivan
1952-53	Montreal Canadiens	Frank Selke	Dick Irvin
1951-52	Detroit Red Wings	Jack Adams	Tommy Ivan
1950-51	Toronto Maple Leafs	Conn Smythe	Joe Primeau
1949-50	Detroit Red Wings	Jack Adams	Tommy Ivan
1948-49	Toronto Maple Leafs	Conn Smythe	Hap Day
1947-48	Toronto Maple Leafs	Conn Smythe	Hap Day
1946-47	Toronto Maple Leafs	Conn Smythe	Hap Day
1945-46	Montreal Canadiens	Tommy Gorman	Dick Irvin
1944-45	Toronto Maple Leafs	Conn Smythe	Hap Day
1943-44	Montreal Canadiens	Tommy Gorman	Dick Irvin
1942-43	Detroit Red Wings	Jack Adams	Jack Adams
1941-42	Toronto Maple Leafs	Conn Smythe	Hap Day
1940-41	Boston Bruins	Art Ross	Cooney Weiland
1939-40	New York Rangers	Lester Patrick	Frank Boucher
1938-39	Boston Bruins	Art Ross	Art Ross
1937-38	Chicago Black Hawks	Bill Stewart	Bill Stewart
1936-37	Detroit Red Wings	Jack Adams	Jack Adams
1935-36	Detroit Red Wings	Jack Adams	Jack Adams
1934-35	Montreal Maroons	Tommy Gorman	Tommy Gorman
1933-34	Chicago Black Hawks	Tommy Gorman	Tommy Gorman
1932-33	New York Rangers	Lester Patrick	Lester Patrick
1931-32	Toronto Maple Leafs	Conn Smythe	Dick Irvin
1930-31	Montreal Canadiens	Cecil Hart	Cecil Hart
1929-30	Montreal Canadiens	Cecil Hart	Cecil Hart
1928-29	Boston Bruins	Art Ross	Cy Denneny
1927-28	New York Rangers	Lester Patrick	Lester Patrick
1926-27	Ottawa Senators	Dave Gill	Dave Gill
1925-26	Montreal Maroons	Eddie Gerard	Eddie Gerard
1924-25	Victoria Cougars	Lester Patrick	Lester Patrick
1923-24	Montreal Canadiens	Leo Dandurand	Leo Dandurand
1922-23	Ottawa Senators	Tommy Gorman	Pete Green
1921-22	Toronto St. Pats	Charlie Querrie	Eddie Powers
1920-21	Ottawa Senators	Tommy Gorman	Pete Green
1919-20	Ottawa Senators	Tommy Gorman	Pete Green
1918-19	a—No decision.		
1917-18	Toronto Arenas	Charlie Querrie	Dick Carroll

a—In the spring of 1919 the Montreal Canadiens traveled to Seattle to meet Seattle, PCHL champions. After five games had been played—teams were tied at 2 wins each and 1 tie—the series was called off by the local Department of Health because of the influenza epidemic and the death from influenza of Joe Hall.

STANLEY CUP WINNERS PRIOR TO FORMATION OF NHL IN 1917

Season	Champions	Manager	Coach
1916-17	Seattle Metropolitans	Pete Muldoon	Pete Muldoon
1915-16	Montreal Canadiens	George Kennedy	George Kennedy
1914-15	Vancouver Millionaires	Frank Patrick	Frank Patrick
1913-14	Toronto Blueshirts	Jack Marshall	Scotty Davidson*
**1912-13	Quebec Bulldogs	M.J. Quinn	Joe Malone*
1911-12	Quebec Bulldogs	M.J. Quinn	C. Nolan
1910-11	Ottawa Senators		Bruce Stuart*
1909-10	Montreal Wanderers	R.R. Boon	Pud Glass*
1908-09	Ottawa Senators		Bruce Stuart*
1907-08	Montreal Wanderers	R.R. Boon	Cecil Blachford
1906-07	Montreal Wanderers (March)	R.R. Boon	Cecil Blachford
1906-07	Kenora Thistles (January)	F.A. Hudson	Tommy Phillips*
1905-06	Montreal Wanderers		
1904-05	Ottawa Silver Seven		A.T. Smith
1903-04	Ottawa Silver Seven		A.T. Smith
1902-03	Ottawa Silver Seven		A.T. Smith
1901-02	Montreal A.A.A.		R.R. Boon*
1900-01	Winnipeg Victorias		
1899-1900	Montreal Shamrocks		H.J. Trihey*
1898-99	Montreal Shamrocks		H.J. Trihey*
1897-98	Montreal Victorias		F. Richardson
1896-97	Montreal Victorias		Mike Grant*
1895-96	Montreal Victorias (December, 1896)		Mike Grant*
1895-96	Winnipeg Victorias (February)		
1894-95	Montreal Victorias		Mike Grant*
1893-94	Montreal A.A.A.		
1892-93	Montreal A.A.A.		

**Victoria defeated Quebec in challenge series. No official recognition.
**In the early years the teams were frequently run by the Captain.* *Indicates Captain.

WHA WORLD TROPHY WINNERS

Season	Champions	Manager	Coach
1973-74	Houston Aeros	James S. Smith	Bill Dineen
1972-73	New England Whalers	Jack Kelley	Jack Kelley

PREVIEW

NHL PREVIEW

Two more games, two more divisions, two more teams. Those are the major changes in the National Hockey League for the 1974-75 season.

After 50 years of routine, the same six teams and the same playoff system, the National Hockey League has started to catch up with leagues in other sports in vast expansion and revitalization programs.

So when the Washington Capitals and Kansas City Scouts begin play this October, they will be the 11th and 12th teams added in a mere eight years. No league has grown as rapidly.

And with Seattle and Denver already ticketed to join the circuit for the 1976 season, the league's structure had to be changed from two to four divisions.

As a result, the NHL's new look will take this form:

Division I
Atlanta
N.Y. Islanders
N.Y. Rangers
Philadelphia

Division II
Detroit
Los Angeles
Montreal
Pittsburgh
Washington

Division III
Chicago
Kansas City
Minnesota
St. Louis
Vancouver

Division IV
Boston
Buffalo
California
Toronto

Another change will be the points system, which will be the determining factor for a team to make the playoffs. The 12 teams that earn the most points will qualify for the playoffs.

Ken Dryden returns to tend goal for Montreal this season.

NHL Vice President Don Ruck predicts this new system will maintain fan interest. "A team isn't going to be hopelessly out of the playoffs after one-third of the season. Every race could go down to the last game," he said.

It will probably keep the players interested, too. A team is not likely to let up if it has clinched first place, because points will determine the home advantage in the playoff quarterfinals. As in the past, however, there will be an incentive for a team to finish atop a division: the first-place team will draw a bye into the second round of the playoffs. The lower teams will play a best-of-3 elimination series before facing the division champs.

So a long road lies ahead; and if the NHL moguls have devised the most beneficial plan, the Stanley Cup playoffs are likely to be more competitive than ever before.

Here is the way each of the 18 teams shape up:

DIVISON I

PHILADELPHIA FLYERS

The Flyers came through the summer expansion draft in excellent shape, despite losing veteran Simon Nolet. Nolet was a sparkplug in the Stanley Cup triumph over the Boston Bruins last season, but was sacrificed to the Kansas City Scouts in order to protect Terry Crisp and Joe Watson.

Philadelphia can expect another solid year in goal from Bernie Parent, another typical high-scoring season from Bobby Clarke, and excellent play from what may be the most tenacious defensive team in hockey.

Ed Van Impe, Moose Dupont, Tom Bladon, and the Watson brothers, Joe and Jim, rarely permit opposing forwards to linger around Parent's goal crease, and that—along with Parent's superior netminding—helped the Cup drive immensely.

The only sad note was the forced retirement of defensive stalwart Barry Ashbee, whose vision will never be the same because a shot by New York defenseman Dale Rolfe struck him in the eye during the playoff semifinals.

Ed Giacomin has been an ironman in goal for the Rangers ever since coming to the club in 1965.

But Coach Fred Shero will find a way to overcome the loss. Young forwards like Rick MacLeish, Bill Barber, Don Saleski and Bill Clement will spark the offense, and the Flyers show every indication of being a Stanley Cup contender for some years to come.

NEW YORK RANGERS

The prediction has been made time and time again, but it now looks as though this could finally be the Rangers' year. New York Coach and General Manager Emile Francis did some house-cleaning during the summer, unloading Vic Hadfield, the high-priced left wing, and picking up brash Derek Sanderson.

The Sanderson move is important. When he wants to be, Sanderson is one of the top faceoff men in the sport; and faceoffs are most important.

In addition, because he is a strong penalty killer, Sanderson could take over this assignment from Walter Tkaczuk, who has been overworked in past seasons. If the controversial center settles down and plays sound hockey for the Rangers, it could make a major difference in the team.

Goalie Ed Giacomin turned in another excellent performance during last year's playoffs and can be expected to do the same this regular season. Right wing Rod Gilbert continues a great career while young left wing Steve Vickers follows suit. Brad Park's superior play will anchor the defense with help from rookie Larry Sacharuk and agressive young forwards Jerry Butler and Burt Wilson.

Maybe this year, the prediction will come true.

ATLANTA FLAMES

No one really expected the Flames to make the playoffs in only their second year of existence. But a good effort by a young team for Coach Boom Boom Geoffrion, surprisingly effective play by goaltenders Phil Myre and Dan Bouchard, and a near award-winning performance by rookie center Tom Lysiak carried the Flames to fourth place in the NHL West Division.

The loss of Al McDonough to the World Hockey Association will hurt—he was their second-leading scorer with 55 points; but 27-goal scorer Jacques Richard, aggressive center Curt Bennett, and 26-goal man Bob Leiter will help overcome McDonough's departure.

It won't be easy to battle stronger teams such as the Rangers and Flyers for division honors, but for a third-year team, the Flames have a glowing future.

NEW YORK ISLANDERS

The word "hapless" haunted the Islanders last season, and rightfully so. The club managed only 19 victories in 78

Dennis Hull of the Chicago Black Hawks.

games—a mere six of them on the road—and scored a league-low 182 goals, or just over 2.3 per game.

Clearly, this team is a few years away from any serious threat to the NHL's powers, but there are bright spots. Defenseman Denis Potvin, the Rookie of the Year, scored 17 goals and added 37 assists to lead team while helping cut the New York goals-against total from a horrifying 347 in 1972-73 to a far more respectable 247 last season.

Billy Harris, another youngster, scored 23 goals; battling Bob Nystrom added 21, and Ralph Stewart 23. Gary Howatt, the Islander policeman, proved himself as a scrapper in his rookie year.

Little Andre St. Laurent was a pleasant surprise, as was Lorne Henning. The steady play of Ed Westfall was no surprise at all.

For the Islanders, it'll be some time before many prizes are won. But this team, someday, will round into shape; and the word "hapless" will be eliminated as a reference.

DIVISION II

DETROIT RED WINGS

Last year's dreadful start spoiled the season for the Red Wings. This year, starting under Coach Alex Delvecchio, things may be different.

Delvecchio has a number of respectable hockey players: Marcel Dionne scored 78 points; Mickey Redmond tallied 51 goals; Nick Libett can finesse or fight with equal ability; Henry Boucha, Guy Charron, Bill Hogaboam and Pierre Jarry are all capable of playing solid hockey. The question mark last year was the defense.

The complaint last year was that many players didn't check as well as they could, putting strain on the defense and the goaltenders. Detroit's 319 goals-against was better only than California's 342.

The acquisition of goaltender Jim Rutherford helped last season, but Delvecchio must concentrate on improving the defense if the Red Wings are to move up in the standings.

LOS ANGELES KINGS

Coach Bob Pulford has done an excellent job with his players, and General Manager Jake Milford has done all he can to give Pulford better players to work with.

Center Gene Carr started to realize his potential, along with other former New York Rangers such as Tom Williams, Juha Widing, Mike Murphy and Sheldon Kannegeisser.

Goaltender Rogatien Vachon teamed with Gary Edwards for a creditable goals-against average of 2.96, good for fifth place among league netminders.

The Kings acquitted themselves well in their playoff series against Chicago; and every Black Hawk will tell you those were five very tough games in the playoff's first round.

Montreal defenseman Guy Lapointe (left) gives Ranger Rod Gilbert a ride as they battle for the puck.

This will be the first full year together for many of the Kings. They should do extremely well once they get to know each other better.

MONTREAL CANADIENS

The acknowledged champion of NHL front-offices is Sam Pollock, who has wrangled more draft choices over more years from more teams than anyone in the league's history. So, every year, the Canadiens are the most popular team to trade with . . . they always have something to offer.

This year was no exception. With the return, after a year's absence, of top goaltender Ken Dryden, Pollock could afford to lose a good one such as Michel Plasse and still have *two* fine backup goalies in Wayne Thomas and Bunny Larocque. The Canadiens finished second to the Boston Bruins last season, and lost to the Rangers in the first round of the playoffs.

Still, they're one of the best clubs in hockey. Yvan Cournoyer still amazes with his speed; Pete Mahovlich can dominate a game. So can Jacques Lemaire, Guy Lafleur, and the group of youngsters that Pollock always pulls out of his hat. Steve Shutt, Murray Wilson, Chuck Lefley and Yvon Lambert are potential stars who will help carry the Canadiens to the top of their division.

The fans in Montreal wouldn't stand for anything else.

PITTSBURGH PENGUINS

Pittsburgh—a disappointing fifth in the West last year—will have a natural leader in Vic Hadfield, who joins former New York Ranger teammates Syl Apps, Ab DeMarco, and Steve Durbano in a Pittsburgh uniform.

When Marc Boileau took over as coach late last season, the players regained the winning formula they had lost, and showed some signs of breaking out of the doldrums.

Right wing Jean Pronovost has been impressive during his four years in the NHL; he scored 40 goals last season—only three fewer than Lowell MacDonald's team-leading total.

The departure of Nick Beverly is no great loss, although if there is one position the Penguins need help, it's on defense. They traded two solid backliners in Darryl Edestrand and Jack Lynch, leaving themselves short of competent rearguards.

WASHINGTON CAPITALS

The Capitals did not get their money's worth at the expan-

Alex Delvecchio, general manager-coach of the Detroit Red Wings.

sion draft last June, but they may have the most impressive uniforms in the league. They are red, white and blue, with stars on the sweater and pants.

There are no stars in the lineup, however. The closest the Caps can come to a potential standout is Greg Joly, a 6-foot-1, 190-pound defenseman who scored 21 goals and added 71 assists for last year's Memorial Cup champs, the Regina Pats in the Western Canada Hockey League. As he enters his rookie season, Joly may face comparison with the early careers of the incomparable Bobby Orr and almost-equally brilliant Brad Park. But he won't be enough to help the Capitals win much in their rookie season.

DIVISION III

CHICAGO BLACK HAWKS

The Black Hawks' annual finish atop the West Division was interrupted last season by the Cup-bound Flyers, but they shouldn't have much difficulty taking the Division III crown.

They are very solid in goal with co-Vezina Trophy winner Tony Esposito and the up man Mike Veisor. Defense is no problem with veterans such as Bill White, Doug Jarrett, Keith Magnuson and young Phil Russell, and their forward crew of Stan Mikita, Dennis Hull, Dick Redmond, Dale Tallon, Jim Pappin, Cliff Koroll and Pit Martin is among the most experienced and solid in the NHL.

Overall, it's very hard to find a weakness in the Black Hawks. They even compiled an outstanding 21-8-10 record on the road. If there has been any letdown by Chicago, it's been in the playoffs. They haven't won the Cup since 1960-61.

KANSAS CITY SCOUTS

The Scouts came away far better than the Capitals from the expansion draft, particularly in goal. Peter McDuffe, formerly of the Rangers and Michel Plasse, formerly of the

Canadiens, will take advantage of the chance to play regularly in this league.

Defensemen like Brent Hughes and Paul Terbenche aren't exactly Norris Trophy candidates, but they'll provide some experience on the backline.

Simon Nolet is a proven performer, and others including Butch Deadmarsh, Gary Croteau, Lynn Powis, Doug Horbul and Randy Rota may play better than most people expect.

MINNESOTA NORTH STARS

The North Stars have tried hard to find a backup man for Cesare Maniago in goal now that Gump Worsley has retired again. But it looks like the position will be filled by Fern Rivard. Rivard could end up with the starting job in goal for awhile if Maniago is slow to recover from off-season knee surgery.

At other positions, there are some fine hockey players on the North Stars. Bill Goldsworthy scored 48 goals; Dennis Hextall scored 20 goals and set up 62 others to lead the team; Danny Grant had another good year with 29-35—64, and J.P. Parise was not far behind.

But former General Manager Wren Blair analyzed the club's problem well last season. "The team is lethargic," he said, "and I don't know if any one stroke of the brush will correct this. We can't put our finger on the reasons, but there are a million reasons why a club goes stale."

And there's no indication things will change this year.

ST. LOUIS BLUES

Last year's St. Louis Blues nearly gave Coach Jean-Guy Talbot a nervous breakdown. This year's team could be easier to handle for new coach Lou Angotti.

The talent is there. Garry Unger's 33-goal season established him as an All-Star, Greg Polis came over from the Penguins to help out at left wing, and rookie John Davidson showed considerable potential with an outstanding 3.08 year in goal.

A 3.08 average will not win the Vezina Trophy, but Davidson showed great agility for a man his size (6-foot-3, 205 pounds), and at just 21 years of age he will be the man the Blues build around in the future.

VANCOUVER CANUCKS

Canuck fans are hoping that the team's new owners will provide a situation more stable than last year when management changed coaches and general managers regularly.

Some people were surprised that a team with many heavy hitters did so little hitting. The lack of aggressiveness hurt because the club lost 43 games.

At one point in the season goaltender Gary Smith walked out. With the defense he was getting, it was hard to blame him. Dennis Ververgaert led the team with 26 goals in his rookie season and Jocelyn Guevremont played well on defense. Chris Oddleifson is one of the league's best on faceoffs, and there are other young players with talent in Vancouver.

Still, a lot of work will have to be done before that talent evolves into a winning team.

DIVISION IV

BOSTON BRUINS

The Bruins unloaded Sanderson, replaced Bep Guidolin as coach with Don Cherry, then took the rest of the summer to regroup forces for another attempt at winning the Stanley Cup. They don't have too far to go.

They lost to Philadelphia in a six-game Cup final after winning the East Division title. Phil Esposito won another scoring championship with 145 points, Bobby Orr was again the best defenseman in the game and scored 122 points, Ken Hodge added 50 goals, leaving mere 30-goal scorers like

Lou Angotti is GM-coach of the St. Louis Blues.

Wayne Cashman, Johnny Bucyk and Bobby Schmautz far behind.

Gilles Gilbert had an outstanding year in goal, but inexperience still showed every once in a while; Terry O'Reilly, Andre Savard and Dave Forbes muscled their way into the lineup and played well, while the hard-hitting defense made Gilbert's job easier.

BUFFALO SABRES

The Sabres may have goalie problems. Dave Dryden jumped to the Chicago Cougars of the WHA, Roger Crozier is in failing health, and their two other goalies, Rocky Farr and Gary Bromley, have a total of 24 games experience in the NHL.

The prospect isn't a pleasant one for Buffalo fans, but there are a lot of young, strong players on the Sabres who may be able to make up for the netminders' inexperience.

The line of Richard Martin, Rene Robert and Gilbert Perreault combined for 202 points last season and would have scored more had Perreault not missed two months with a broken leg. The young, hard-hitting defense of Mike Robitaille, Larry Carriere, Jerry Korab (who can also play wing) and Jim Schoenfeld is very strong, too.

If Schoenfeld has completely recovered from his back injury, if Perreault can keep from getting hurt, and Farr and Bromley play like major leaguers, the Sabres can be a power in Division IV.

CALIFORNIA SEALS

Instead of trying to improve on their dismal last-place record of last season, the Seals seemingly took a couple of steps backward by trading Ivan Boldirev, Reg Leach, and Walt McKechnie.

Drafting defenseman Jim Neilson will help the weak defense, but Neilson can't work miracles—and that's exactly what the Seals need.

Sid Abel, general manager of the NHL's new Kansas City Scouts.

Coach Marshall Johnston and goaltender Gilles Meloche deserve far better support than they have gotten. Meloche kept the Seals in half of the games they eventually lost.

The Seals have done poorly at the gate, prompting one player to remark, "There are 500,000 Canadians in this city who came to Oakland to get away from hockey."

TORONTO MAPLE LEAFS

The Leafs lost a few players in the off-season, and it might hurt them in the long run. Mike Pelyk and Paul Henderson jumped to the World Hockey Association, Denis Dupere was lost to Washington in the expansion draft, and goalie Ed Johnston was traded to the St. Louis Blues. Toronto still has Doug Favell and Dunc Wilson for the goaltending chores and other young forwards to cover up for the loss of the 31-year-old Henderson. However, Pelyk was one of the harder hitters on the Toronto backline.

Center Darryl Sittler had a marvelous year last season with 38 goals and 46 assists, and veteran Norm Ullman chipped in with 69 points. Swedish imports Inge Hammarstrom and Borje Salming played very well, too.

But this year is not "the year" for the Maple Leafs, who could use some help at forward. The fans might get a bit annoyed at paying a $12 top for tickets, an increase of more than $4.

WHA PREVIEW

Five of the World Hockey Association's 14 teams are playing in new cities this season, nearly half of the teams have moved to new arenas, and now there are three divisions instead of two.

The Los Angeles Sharks have moved to Detroit and changed their name to the Michigan Stags. They'll play their games at Cobo Arena (home of the National Basketball Association Pistons) and their new coach is Johnny Wilson.

The New York Raiders are no longer the New York Golden Blades or even the Jersey Knights. They have moved to the West Coast, and will reside at the San Diego Sports Arena as the San Diego Mariners.

The New England Whalers have moved, too—but only from Boston to Hartford, Conn.

And there are two new teams: the Phoenix Roadrunners and the Indianapolis Racers.

Meanwhile, the Edmonton Oilers have moved into a beautiful new arena and will host this year's All-Star game; the Toronto Toros have left tiny Varsity Stadium for venerable Maple Leaf Gardens, and the Cleveland Crusaders have shifted from the dingy Cleveland Arena to an impressive building called The Coliseum.

Also, there'll be the new divisional breakdown, which will look like this:

West Division	Canadian Division	East Division
Houston	Edmonton	Cleveland
Michigan	Quebec	Chicago
Minnesota	Toronto	Indianapolis
Phoenix	Vancouver	New England
San Diego	Winnipeg	

Under this new concept, the first two teams from each division will make the playoffs, as will two "wild card" teams.

The Cincinnati Stingers, who will join the league in 1975, probably will fill out the East Division.

Other WHA developments include a seven-game Team Canada vs. Russia series and the possible phasing out of the center red line in an effort to speed up the game.

The Team Canada series has produced "instant respectability" for this third-year league, according to President Dennis Murphy. "This is an opportunity for us to show our game to the world," Murphy added.

There is a chance the red line will be abolished. The change was to be tried during the exhibition schedule. Forward passes would be permitted from the defending zone to the blue line of the offensive zone—a move designed to further open up an already wide-open game.

Western Division

HOUSTON AEROS

The Aeros finished first in just about everything last season. That's no surprise, really. The people of Texas won't put up with any less than that for too long.

Gordie Howe made a fine comeback and was in the running for WHA Rookie of the Year honors until his son Mark came along and stole it. Papa Gordie had to settle for the Most Valuable Player award after leading Houston scorers with 31 goals and 69 assists for 100 points.

Young Mark Howe finished as the WHA's second-best rookie scorer with 38 goals and 41 assists for 79 points—just one less than teammate Andre Hinse.

Houston's Don McLeod cruised away with the award as top goaltender, finishing with a 2.57 goals-against average, 33 wins in 49 games, and three shutouts. With McLeod, Wayne Rutledge and Ron Grahame in nets behind a solid defense, the Aeros gave up the fewest goals in the league: 219.

Goalie Dave Dryden jumped from Buffalo of the NHL to Chicago of the WHA for the 1974 season.

With all that and more going for them this year (except possibly for Papa Gordie, who may just sit in the front office this year), there's no reason the Aeros shouldn't repeat as West Division champs.

MINNESOTA FIGHTING SAINTS

If there is to be any serious competition for the Aeros, it probably will be provided by the Fighting Saints, who finished second in the West with 90 points last season.

Mike Walton went on a mind-boggling spree as the season entered its stretch run and at one point had scored 11 goals in just three games. He carried the Saints to their second-place finish, finishing with a league-leading 117 points—including 57 goals.

Overlooked in Walton's 117-point total was a most impressive 95 points by Wayne Connelly. Not far behind in third was George Morrison at 78 points. There were four teams in the league last year whose scoring leaders didn't have that many points.

The Saints appear to have a weakness on the defensive end, though, having allowed 275 goals last season. Mike Curran made the All-Star team and young John Garrett wasn't far behind, but it seemed there were a few too many mistakes at the blue line. The Saints might cut back on their free-wheeling style this year in order to concentrate more on defense.

Too much offense often leads to not enough defense. And that, the coaches will tell you, doesn't win championships.

SAN DIEGO MARINERS

It's hard to believe a last-place team could be so good, but the San Diego Mariners could have made the playoffs with a break here or there.

If there's one thing this club hasn't gotten—ever—it's a break. They lead the league in bad luck and very little else.

Last season was wasted virtually from the first week on. When the owners couldn't meet their payroll, the team was moved to Jersey and most of the players commuted from their New York homes for every game.

Andre Lacroix finished second only to Walton among WHA scorers, though, and rookie defenseman Kevin Morrison broke a couple of records by scoring 24 goals and 43 assists for 67 points.

The play of those two was one of the few bright spots in a dismal season for Jersey (as they were called), and it's hard to believe Lacroix even stayed with the team after a $44,000 bonus check somehow fell into the hands of the now-ousted New York owners.

Still, Lacroix showed a lot of class, stayed with the team, and fell just six points short of winning a second straight scoring title. Joe Junkin played well in goal for the Knights and if a decent backup goalie can be obtained this year's Mariners could make some progress.

They have a solid group of forwards including veterans like Mike Laughton, Brian Bradley, Wayne Rivers, Norm Ferguson and Don Herriman; they have one of the league's best defensemen in Ken Block, although few other backliners are worth mentioning.

A trade or two could work wonders for the Mariners. A couple of breaks wouldn't hurt, either.

MICHIGAN STAGS

Admittedly, the Jersey Knights had a bad year last season. The Los Angeles Sharks (now the Stags) were worse. And they had fewer excuses.

In 78 games they got 50 points, lost 31 of 39 road games, and scored a paltry 239 goals—just over three per game—while allowing 339, or 4.3 per game.

Marc Tardif scored 40 goals but had just 30 assists to lead Sharks scorers, while attendance at the 14,700-seat Los Angeles Sports Arena dropped by 25,000.

Statistically, they were the worst club in the league. And there was little indication things would improve despite a new coach in Johnny Wilson and a new goalie in ex-NHLer

Gerry Desjardins.

The Stags need help in every department, and even then, there's little hope for improvement this year.

PHOENIX ROADRUNNERS

The Roadrunners will be a combination of players from last year's Western Hockey League entry of the same name and a couple of players from the Cincinnati franchise, who'll spend the year in Phoenix to pass time until the Stingers join the league.

Last year's club carried off its second consecutive Western League championship, becoming the only team in the league's history to win two league and playoff titles back-to-back.

Look for colorful Howie Young to be among the most popular of the Phoenix players, although Cincinnati draft choice Dennis Sobchuk will be of great value to the Phoenix offense.

The 20-year-old Sobchuk scored 191 goals and 416 points in three years with the Regina Pats and signed a 10-year, $1.7 million contract with the Stingers. He'll be a valued addition to the Roadrunners this year, though, and the Phoenix fans will be ready to embrace him.

The Roadrunners averaged 8,321 spectators for 43 games in the WHL last season, and should improve on that this year with what could be a surprisingly tough entry.

Two players won't carry a team, of course, but Gary Kurt might reach the potential he has been seeking in goal the last couple of years, Steve King (drafted from Toronto) will help, as will others like Bob Jones, Jack Gibson, Ted Hodgson, and Michel Plante.

CANADIAN DIVISION

TORONTO TOROS

The Toros, with Paul Henderson and Frank Mahovlich, appear likely to top the Canadian Division. Experts feel the

Toros own the league's best young goaltender in Gilles Gratton, and with the addition of these two name players from the National Hockey League, there is every chance of a division title.

Toronto finished a close second to New England in the East Division last year, and many were surprised when the Chicago Cougars eliminated them in the playoff semifinals. Wayne "Swoop" Carleton again led the Toros in scoring with 92 points (including 37 goals) while the young club turned balanced scoring and adequate defense into a run for the title.

Nine Toros scored more than 20 goals (eight were over 20 on the champion Aeros) and with Henderson and Mahovlich, those numbers figure to increase. An adequate backup goalie to Gratton (one younger than 39-year-old Les Binkley) could send this team on its way.

EDMONTON OILERS

The Oilers will have Jacques Plante between the pipes as the season opens. The 45-year-old netminder resigned his job as coach and general manager of the Quebec Nordiques to join the Oilers as a player.

People are still wondering what happened to the Oilers last year, after they broke out of the gate with a 12-1 record over the first 13 games.

It appears they just ran out of steam and only held off the Winnipeg Jets for third place in the West on the strength of the early-season spurt.

Still Ron Climie scored consistently for Edmonton, finishing with 38 goals and 74 points, and controversial Jim Harrison (who once scored three goals and seven assists for 10 points in a single game) helped when he wasn't injured.

Alan Hamilton was steady on defense and Jack Norris was stable in the Edmonton nets. With Norris gone to the Racers, though, the Oilers need somebody to share the load with Plante, who says he could play 50 games but really can't.

Defenseman Ted Green (6) of the New England Whalers wears a helmet after near-tragic accident in 1969.

NORTHLAND

QUEBEC NORDIQUES

The Nordiques were a major disappointment last season, after most had figured them to be one of the strong clubs all the way through the playoffs.

It isn't that they had a bad year by any means. The Cougars managed to beat them out by a mere point for fourth place and the final playoff spot. But it was assumed they'd at least make the playoffs.

If there is one strength in Quebec, it is in goal. Michel Deguise and Richard Brodeur averaged 3.29 and 3.32 respectively, but both are youngsters and figure to be very strong this season. Serge Aubry, the third Quebec goaltender, is no slouch, either.

Serge Bernier had a fine year (37 goals, 49 assists) for the Nordiques as did Bob Guindon and Andre Gaudette, who tied for second place among team scorers with 68 points each.

Plante laid a creditable groundwork in the French-speaking North, signing Bernier, Deguise, defenseman Dale Hoganson and Rejean Houle for the Nordiques. A road record of 13-26-0 prevented them from doing better.

VANCOUVER BLAZERS

Vancouver is promising, too, and it is strange that they did as poorly as they did. Despite Danny Lawson's 50-goal year, the defense permitted a horrifying 345 goals and the Blazers won a paltry eight of 39 games away from home.

The shining star in the Vancouver future is center Claude St. Sauveur, who tore up the old Eastern Hockey League before joining the Blazers for full-time duty last season. St. Sauveur scored 38 goals as a rookie and finished with 68 points.

Veteran Bryan Campbell had a solid year as well, tying Lawson for the scoring lead with 88 points. And don't forget John McKenzie, who is still part of the fire that makes up the Blazers.

But that goals-against average will have to come down, and the defense is too young and inexperienced to do it. Also

Peter Donnelly just isn't strong enough to carry the weight alone. Yves Archambault and Danny Sullivan might just take Donnelly's starting job away.

It's going to be tough for the Blazers unless new General Manager Joe Crozier makes a trade or two . . . and there isn't a lot to trade on this club.

WINNIPEG JETS

It was a frustrating year for Bobby Hull's Jets, who never managed to get off the ground. It seems as though the talent is there (how could it help but be there with a player of Hull's caliber?) but Winnipeg just didn't have the horses to beat powerful Houston in the first round of the playoffs.

The loss of Fran Huck was something of a surprise, as the little playmaker seemed to have found a spot on Hull's line. Still Chris Bordeleau proved himself one of the league's better centers, Norm Beaudin made a good contribution and Ernie Wakely continued his standout goaltending.

There may be too many "lightweights" on the Jets—too many guys who don't do enough. Maybe some trades should be made.

EAST DIVISION

CHICAGO COUGARS

The Cougars were last season's Cinderella team, and a great deal of the credit rests with player-coach Pat Stapleton and the outstanding play of center Ralph Backstrom. These two walked into training camp, established their leadership on this club, and really obtained every ounce of performance from start to finish.

The result, of course, was the World Cup finals, a Defenseman of the Year award for Stapleton and Sportsmanlike Player of the Year award for Backstrom. They deserved it and more.

Others who deserve praise are tough Rosaire Paiement, whose 73 points were 15 fewer than Backstrom's leading total, goaltender Cam Newton, who compiled a 3.12 goals-against average in this wide-open league, and others who produced a solid team effort.

The other teams in this division are beatable, and the Cougars might just finish at the top after sneaking into fourth place in 1973-74 following a cellar finish in the West the year before.

NEW ENGLAND WHALERS

The Whalers swept to their second consecutive East Division title last season, then got taken out by the Cougars in the first round of the playoffs. Maybe they were a little complacent; first place was sewn up early in the season, and maybe the pressure surprised the Whalers. There were problems, such as the smaller crowds at Boston Garden and the shift to Hartford, but it seems they shouldn't have mattered.

Al Smith played some excellent goal for the Whalers, finishing with a 3.08 goals-against average, and his defense—again—was superior, finishing second to Houston's record with 260 goals-against.

It's hard to find a better defense than Jim Dorey, Ted Green, Brad Selwood and Rick Ley. And their crop of forwards like Larry Pleau, John French, Tim Sheehy and Tom Webster is the kind that can win championships. They proved that in the 1972-73 season.

CLEVELAND CRUSADERS

The Crusaders move into a spanking new building this year and it would please owner Nick Mileti no end if he could provide his fans with a World Cup winner. The acquisition of Al McDonough from the Atlanta Flames and Richie Leduc from the American Hockey League Boston Braves is a fine dividend already.

Cleveland is a very strong hockey club. They've got the top goaltender in Gerry Cheevers (even though he finished second statistically to Houston's McLeod, Cheevers played in 59 games—11 more than McLeod and anybody else in the WHA). He also led in shutouts last season with four.

Beyond that, there are some fine forwards like veteran Gary Jarrett and Ron Ward. Jarrett finished with 71 points, while Ward made Cleveland his third team of the season but finished second in scoring with 61 points. Talented forwards like Jim Wiste, Gerry Pinder, Skip Krake and young Tom Edur provide a solid nucleus to help out the defense anchored by Paul Schmyr.

Shmyr, at 27, has obtained the reputation as the league's best defenseman. Few are inclined to argue, and he is continually improving with each season. He's one of the top hitters in hockey.

INDIANAPOLIS RACERS

The Racers appear to be stressing defense in their first year of operation. Three of the first players they signed were goaltenders.

Ed Dyck jumped the Vancouver Canucks of the National Hockey League to join the Racers, then Edmonton's Jack Norris was obtained in a trade for future considerations. Later, the Racers obtained goalie Gerry Gray in a future considerations trade with the New England Whalers.

Not surprisingly, Indianapolis didn't draft a netminder in the expansion selections. What they did pick were players like Edmonton's Brian McKenzie, Bobby Whitlock of Michigan's Stags, Yves Bergeron from Quebec, Bobby Sicinski of Chicago and Tommy Williams of New England.

Those are the kind of marginally talented players an expansion team has to work with in its first year. The Racers won't go anyplace fast, but there's time and room for improvement.

The loss of Johnny Wilson to Michigan would have been a more staggering blow if he had already begun work with the players. But because it happened early in the offseason, it shouldn't prove any problem. There'll be enough other problems for the Racers to worry about.

EXPANSION DRAFTS

Like giant amoebas, the National Hockey League and World Hockey Association reproduced themselves last summer, each adding two new clubs. That swelled NHL membership to 18 teams and the WHA to 14.

Kansas City and Washington were the new NHL clubs added with Indianapolis and Phoenix joining the WHA. To stock the new teams, the older clubs were permitted to protect their best 15 players and two goalies, with their new partners given the pick of the leftovers. The pickings, especially in the NHL draft, weren't exactly generous.

Most of the established clubs entered into arrangements with the new teams to assure that certain available players would not be picked. That is how you can explain the new clubs in the NHL passing over established available names like Ted Harris, Joe Watson, Claude Larose, Terry Crisp, Bob Nevin and Roger Crozier and selecting instead unknown players like Normand Dube, Tom Peluso, Butch Deadmarsh, Larry Bolonchuck, Larry Fullan and Bob Collyard.

The best-known players drafted in the NHL expansion were Kansas City's Simon Nolet, a 19-goal scorer for Philadelphia, and Washington's Denis Dupere, who had eight goals for Toronto.

The new WHA clubs faired somewhat better. Phoenix came up with Bob Jones, who had 17 goals and 45 points for Jersey, and Jack Gibson, a 16-goal scorer for Toronto. Three of Indianapolis' choices, Bob Whitlock, Steve Cardwell and Tom Williams, all scored 20 or more goals in 1973-74.

The drafts might be best summed up by what General Manager Bud Poile had said in 1970 when he made Vancouver's expansion selections. "I came in looking for a life raft," said Poile, "and they threw me an anchor."

NHL EXPANSION DRAFT

KANSAS CITY SCOUTS

Player	Position	Drafted From	1973-74 Record
Michel Plasse	Goal	Montreal	4.08
Peter McDuffe	Goal	NY Rangers	3.51*
Brent Hughes	Defense	Detroit	1-21—22
Paul Terbenche	Defense	Buffalo	2-12—14
Chris Evans	Defense	Detroit	4-9—13
Bryan Lefley	Defense	NY Islanders	8-36—44*
Kerry Ketter	Defense	Atlanta	5-20—25*
Ken Murray	Defense	Detroit	3-15—18*
Dennis Patterson	Defense	Minnesota	8-25—33*
Simon Nolet	Forward	Philadelphia	19-17—36
Butch Deadmarsh	Forward	Atlanta	6-1—7
Gary Coalter	Forward	California	38-31—69*
Gary Croteau	Forward	California	14-21—35
Randy Rota	Forward	Los Angeles	10-6—16
John Wright	Forward	St. Louis	6-9—15
Lynn Powis	Forward	Chicago	8-13—21
Ted Snell	Forward	Pittsburgh	4-12—16
Robin Burns	Forward	Pittsburgh	31-35—66*
Tom Peluso	Forward	Chicago	19-19—38*
Normand Dube	Forward	Los Angeles	32-21—53*
Richard Lemieux	Forward	Vancouver	5-17—22
Dave Hudson	Forward	NY Islanders	2-10—12
Ed Gilbert	Forward	Montreal	30-44—74*
Doug Horbul	Forward	NY Rangers	34-29—63*

*Minor League Statistics

WASHINGTON CAPITALS

Player	Position	Drafted From	1973-74 Record
Ron Low	Goal	Toronto	3.16*
Michel Belhumeur	Goal	Philadelphia	4.18*
Yvon Labre	Defense	Pittsburgh	6-23—29*
Gordon Smith	Defense	Los Angeles	13-54—67*
Joe Lundrigan	Defense	Toronto	7-34—41*
Mike Bloom	Defense	Boston	25-44—69*
Bill Mikkelson	Defense	NY Islanders	1-21—22*
Larry Bolonchuck	Defense	Vancouver	6-27—33*
Murray Anderson	Defense	Minnesota	9-34—43*
Dave Kryskow	Forward	Chicago	7-12—19
Mike Lampman	Forward	Vancouver	14-20—34*

Pete Laframboise	Forward	California	7-7—14
Bob Gryp	Forward	Boston	30-18—48*
Steve Atkinson	Forward	Buffalo	6-10—16
Bruce Cowick	Forward	Philadelphia	14-7—21*
Denis Dupere	Forward	Toronto	8-9—17
Randy Wyrozub	Forward	Buffalo	22-35—57*
Gordon Brooks	Forward	St. Louis	6-8—14
Bob Collyard	Forward	St. Louis	27-47—74*
Ron Anderson	Forward	Boston	24-31—55*
Lew Morrison	Forward	Atlanta	1-4—5
Steve West	Forward	Minnesota	50-60—110*
Larry Fullan	Forward	Montreal	37-47—84*
Jack Egers	Forward	NY Rangers	1-4—5

*Minor League Statistics

WHA EXPANSION DRAFT

PHOENIX ROADRUNNERS

Player	Position	Drafted From	1973-74 Record
Gary Kurt	Goal	San Diego	4.17
Gerry Odrowski	Defense	Michigan	4-32—36
Ted Hodgson	Forward	Michigan	3-11—14
Bill Young	Forward	Michigan	9-12—21
Dick Pumple	Forward	Cleveland	2-2—4
Bob Jones	Forward	San Diego	17-28—45
Bernie Blanchette	Forward	Edmonton	
Steve King	Forward	Toronto	13-21—34
Dick Sarrazin	Forward	Chicago	
Terry Ryan	Forward	Minnesota	
Ron Anderson	Defense	Chicago	0-0—0
Jack Gibson	Forward	Toronto	16-9—25
Jim McMasters	Forward	Cleveland	0-0—0
Michael Plante	Forward	Vancouver	3-2—5
Steve Warr	Forward	Toronto	

INDIANAPOLIS RACERS

Player	Position	Drafted From	1973-74 Record
Brian McKenzie	Forward	Edmonton	18-20—38
Bob Fitchner	Forward	Edmonton	1-2—3
Bob Whitlock	Forward	Michigan	20-29—49
Bob Ash	Defense	Winnipeg	2-18—20

Bob Sicinski	Forward	Chicago	11-29—40
Rychard Campeau	Defense	Vancouver	0-0—0
Roger Cote	Defense	Edmonton	0-3—3
Steve Cardwell	Forward	Minnesota	23-23—46
Jim Hargreaves	Defense	Winnipeg	1-4—5
Mike Archambault	Forward	Quebec	
Ken Desjardine	Defense	Quebec	2-9—11
Billy Orr	Defense	Toronto	3-9—12
Cal Swenson	Forward	Winnipeg	5-4—9
Yves Bergeron	Forward	Quebec	
Pierre Henry	Forward	Vancouver	
Ron Morgan	Forward	Cleveland	
Tom Williams	Forward	New England	21-37—58

HALL OF FAME

Located on the grounds of the Canadian National Exhibition, just a few minutes from downtown Toronto, the Hockey Hall of Fame honors almost 200 players, builders and referees whose contributions have made hockey one of the world's greatest sports.

All eras of the game's history are represented from the legendary Frank McGee, who once scored 14 goals in a single Stanley Cup game in 1905, to fiery Maurice "The Rocket" Richard, the first man to score 50 goals in a single season, to Gordie Howe, hockey's all-time highest scorer. They are among the nearly 150 players enshrined.

The builders' section includes the Patrick brothers, Frank and Lester, who spread hockey across North America with the introduction of the Pacific Coast Hockey League and built Canada's first artificial hockey rinks.

Among the referees honored are Mickey Ion, whose famous advice to a young official reminded the rookie that "there are 20,000 people in this building and the only one of them who's sane is you."

Three members have been selected for profiling here —Jean Beliveau to represent the players, Clarence Campbell to represent builders and Bill Chadwick to represent referees.

JEAN BELIVEAU

There always has been a certain majesty about Jean Beliveau. It is an aura that surrounded him on the ice in 18 seasons as an outstanding center ice man for the Montreal Canadiens and still does today in his position as a vice president of the club.

Montreal fans demand hockey excellence. There are no more critical fans in any city than those in the capital of French Canada. They boo at the drop of a puck. But never in his nearly two decades with the Canadiens did Beliveau hear catcalls. He just wasn't the kind of player you could boo.

Beliveau, a strapping 6-foot-3, 205-pound bull of a hockey player, scored 507 career goals with Montreal. His nickname *Le Gros Bill,* was a tribute to his size. He was a seemingly indestructible giant, the acknowledged leader of the Canadiens and for the last 10 years of his career, captain of the club.

Twice, Beliveau won the Hart Trophy as the NHL's Most Valuable Player. He was the league scoring champion in 1955-56 when he totaled 88 points, including a career-high 47 goals; and in 1965 he was the first winner of the Conn Smythe Trophy as playoff MVP. That was one of 10 years in which Beliveau played on a Stanley Cup championship team.

Traditionally, the Canadiens would turn to Beliveau to lead them and, traditionally, big Jean would do just that. His last active season was 1971 and he went out in a blaze of glory, pacing the Canadiens to another Cup and setting a playoff record of 16 assists while doing it.

A year later, the Hall of Fame selection committee waived the traditional five-year waiting period and inducted Jean Beliveau.

CLARENCE CAMPBELL

When Clarence Campbell became president of the National Hockey League in 1946, it had six teams, with Chicago marking its western outpost and no team farther south than New York. In 1974, with Campbell still president, the NHL welcomed its 17th and 18th member clubs—Kansas City and Washington, D.C.—and stretched as far west as Los Angeles and as far south as Atlanta. That kind of growth is a tribute to the leadership that Campbell has provided to the league.

Campbell presided over the most ambitious expansion program in the history of sports—the wholesale addition of

Clarence Campbell, president of the NHL.

six new franchises to the NHL in 1967. Subsequently, the league added two teams in 1970, two more in 1972 and now two more in 1974.

A brilliant attorney, Campbell has served hockey not only as an executive, but also, for many years, as a referee before turning his attention to the administrative side of the game.

Campbell, born and raised in Canada's western prairie land, graduated from the University of Alberta and then from Oxford University in England. He was a Rhodes Scholar and commanded the 4th Canadian Armed Division during World War Two. After the war, he served with the Canadian War Crimes Unit at the Nuremburg Trials.

Perhaps his proudest accomplishment in Campbell's tenure as NHL president was the introduction and implementation of the NHL pension system, considered one of the finest in professional sports.

His forceful leadership of the league was recognized in 1966 by his induction into the Hall of Fame, and emphasized again in 1972 when he won the Lester Patrick Trophy for service to hockey in the United States.

BILL CHADWICK

Born and raised in New York City, Bill Chadwick was an American who made it big in the Canadian game of ice hockey.

Chadwick learned his hockey on the frozen ponds and rinks of the city, developing into a top amateur player. Then an accident on the ice cost him the sight in one eye. Even after that, he continued to play hockey in the Eastern League for Tom Lockhart's New York Rovers.

He was sitting out another injury when Lockhart asked him to substitute for a referee who had been sidetracked by transportation difficulties. Chadwick agreed and thus launched one of the most successful officiating careers in sports.

Lockhart hired Chadwick as a full-time referee for the EHL and two years later he moved up to the National League, first as a linesman and then as a referee. He spent 16 years in the NHL, 14 of them as a referee, and is credited with developing the hand signals used to indicate penalty violations.

Chadwick quickly became acknowledged as the league's top referee and officiated in an all-time record 105 Stanley Cup games. He was known as an impartial referee and when he retired in 1955, the league offered him the position of supervisor of officials. But he chose to turn to private industry instead.

He was elected to the Hall of Fame in 1964, and a few years later, he returned to the hockey scene as a broadcaster for the New York Rangers.

HOCKEY HALL OF FAME
PLAYERS

Sid Abel
Jack Adams
Syl Apps
Don Bain
Hobey Baker
Marty Barry
Jean Beliveau
Clint Benedict
Doug Bentley
Max Bentley
Toe Blake
Dickie Boon
Butch Bouchard
Frank Boucher
Buck Boucher
Russell Bowie
Frank Brimsek
Punch Broadbent
Turk Broda
Billy Burch
Harry Cameron
King Clancy
Dit Clapper
Sprague Cleghorn
Neil Colville
Charlie Conacher
Alex Connell
Bill Cook
Art Coulter
Bill Cowley
Rusty Crawford
Jack Darragh
Scotty Davidson
Hap Day
Cy Denneny
Charles Drinkwater
Tom Dunderdale
Bill Durnan
Red Dutton
Babe Dye
Arthur Farrell
Frank Foyston
Frank Fredrickson
Bill Gadsby
Chuck Gardiner
Herb Gardiner
Jimmy Gardner
Bernie Geoffrion
Eddie Gerard
Billy Gilmour
Ebbie Goodfellow
Moose Goheen
Mike Grant
Shorty Green
Si Griffis
Joe Hall
George Hainsworth
Doug Harvey
George Hay
Riley Hern
Bryan Hextall
Hap Holmes
Tom Hooper
Red Horner
Gordie Howe
Syd Howe
John Hutton
Harry Hyland

Hall of Famer
Jean Beliveau.

James Irvin
Harvey Jackson
Moose Johnson
Ching Johnson
Tom Johnson
Aurel Joliat
Duke Keats
Red Kelly
Ted Kennedy
Elmer Lach
Newsy Lalonde
Jack Laviolette
Hugh Lehman
Percy Leseur
Ted Lindsay
Mickey MacKay
Sylvio Mantha
Joe Malone
Jack Marshall
Steamer Maxwell
Frank McGee
Billy McGimsie
George McNamara
Dickie Moore
Paddy Moran
Howie Morenz
Bill Mosienko
Frank Nighbor
Reg Noble
Harry Oliver
Lester Patrick
Tom Phillips
Didier Pitre
Babe Pratt
Joe Primeau
Harvey Pulford
Frank Rankin
Chuck Rayner
Ken Reardon
Maurice Richard
George Richardson
Gordon Roberts
Art Ross
Blair Russell
Ernie Russell
Jack Ruttan
Terry Sawchuk
Fred Scanlan
Milt Schmidt
Sweeney Schriner
Earl Seibert
Oliver Seibert
Eddie Shore
Babe Siebert
Joe Simpson
Alf Smith
Hooley Smith
Thomas Smith
Barney Stanley
Jack Stewart
Nels Stewart
Bruce Stuart
Hod Stuart
Cyclone Taylor
Harry Trihey
Tiny Thompson
Georges Vezina
Marty Walsh
Jack Walker
Harry Watson
Harry Westwick
Cooney Weiland
Fred Whitcroft
Phat Wilson
Roy Worters

BUILDERS

Lord Stanley of Preston
Charles F. Adams
Weston W. Adams
Thomas Ahearn
Sir Montagu Allan
Goerge V. Brown
Walter Brown
Frank Calder
Clarence S. Campbell
Angus D. Campbell
Leo Dandurand
Frank Dilio
George S. Dudley
James A. Dunn
Thomas Gorman
Charles Hay
William A. Hewitt
Foster Hewitt
James Hendy
Fred Hume
Tommy Ivan
John Reed Kilpatrick
Al Leader
Robert LeBel
Tom Lockhart
Paul Loicq
Hartland de M. Molson
Frederic McLaughlin
Francis Nelson
Bruce A. Norris
James Norris Sr.
James D. Norris
William M. Northey
J. Ambrose O'Brien
Frank Patrick
Allan W. Pickard
Donat Raymond
John Ross Robertson
Claude C. Robinson
Frank J. Selke
Frank D. Smith
Conn Smythe
James T. Sutherland
Lloyd Turner
Carl Voss
Arthur W. Wirtz
Fred Waghorne

REFEREES

Bill Chadwick
Chaucer Elliot
Bobby Hewitson
Mickey Ion
Mike Rodden
Red Storey
Cooper Smeaton
Frank Udvari

ABOUT THE AUTHOR

Hal Bock, hockey editor of The Associated Press, has authored four major books on the sport. The most recent among them were The Big Whistle, the autobiography of Bill Chadwick, and Save! Hockey's Brave Goalies. He is also a contributing editor to the magazine Hockey Sports Stars of 1975, and holds the same position on Pyramid's popular bi-monthly magazine, Sports Today.